School of the Sea

School of the Sea

1937–1946

Stephen A. Richardson

WHITTLES PUBLISHING

Published by
Whittles Publishing,
Dunbeath,
Caithness KW6 6EY,
Scotland, UK
www.whittlespublishing.com

Front cover image: Convoy gathering in Bedford Basin, Halifax Harbour
(Reproduced with kind permission from the Maritime Command
Museum and Department of National Defence, Canada)

Every effort has been made to trace copyright holders and to obtain their permission
for the use of copyright material. The publisher would be grateful if notified of any
amendments that should be incorporated in future reprints or editions of this book.

Printed by Bell & Bain Ltd., Glasgow

To my shipmates who were my teachers

Contents

Acknowledgements

I found it a difficult and painful process in writing this book to cut out large sections of my sea diaries of over 1000 pages. I am particularly indebted to my wife, Marion, who read the many drafts of the book, suggested where to cut, and cleaned up my spelling and grammar. John and Laurette Rindlaub, Chris Lyman and David Richardson helped with the cutting and made many helpful suggestions. Margo Harvey did the final editing. I am grateful to them all for their help. I want to thank Linsey Gullon, at Whittles Publishing who has been of great help in the final preparation of the book.

Foreword by Tony Lane

Every writer needs other writers. I was acutely aware of this when in 1985 I was in the preliminary stages of research for an eventual book, *The Merchant Seaman's War*. I needed to get inside the everyday experience of the Second World War's seafarers and hoped – with little optimism – that I might find a diary which embraced wartime and pre-war years. Amazingly, I struck gold! Within weeks of an appeal published in a British seamen's union journal, Stephen Richardson wrote from the USA to say that between the years of 1937, when he first went to sea as an indentured apprentice, and 1946, by which time he had qualified as a master mariner, he had kept a daily diary.

The early pages describe a picture of peacetime life aboard the *Elysia*, a combined passenger and cargo ship, as seen through the eyes of a young apprentice. *Elysia* was on the run between Britain and India and life aboard had changed little since she was designed and built in 1908. Scattered through these pages there are increasing references to the threat of war.

The main body of the diaries covers the span of World War II and the influence the war had on daily life at sea while Stephen was an apprentice on *Elysia* and then an officer on cargo ships. The final pages of the diary tell of the ending of the war and the return to peacetime conditions at sea. The original diary of 1000+ handwritten pages sits now in Liverpool's, Merseyside Maritime Museum. Stephen has skilfully edited his original diary to clear out the inevitable repetitions and redundancies and produced a book which captures like no other every dimension of daily life as seen through the perceptive eyes of a young, Quaker-educated merchant seaman. Extensive and continuous records of everyday life have been kept many times by prominent people with a view to shaping the view that posterity might have of them. Stephen Richardson's record has none of this self-centredness. This diary has no axe to grind, no actions to justify. Genuinely disinterested, it is precisely the sort of record that is immensely important for enhancing our understanding of human affairs.

For the book I was preparing to write, the wartime diaries were central to my interests. During the war years of its writing some 30,000 merchant seamen, of many different nationalities, sailing on British-managed ships lost their lives on the 4800 ships sunk or damaged beyond repair. Stephen Richardson, like the thousands of others who survived the war, experienced the dramas and the mundane routines of shipboard society. I found it easy to identify with the diary's descriptions of and commentaries on life at sea, with the yearning for connectedness with the world beyond the ocean-bounded ship. I too had been an indentured apprentice, albeit starting some eighteen years later, and I had also struggled as a young officer to reach and embrace a wider world. Once we had met, Stephen and I became friends immediately. But it wasn't the friendship that made me urge him to find a way of putting his diary into a form that would make it publishable – it was my knowledge of how much was missing from the existing literature where wartime experiences consisted mainly of danger, excitement and death.

There are a good number of books written by men who were young seamen in the Second World War. With just one notable exception – Morris Beckman's *Atlantic Roulette* – they are focused on the high dramas of attacks by submarine or surface raider and the subsequent survival of those who managed to escape in boats and rafts. When I began my research I was looking for accounts of life where the dramatic and the mundane were in the same frame. In the introduction to my book, when it finally emerged after five years of digging and weeding, I wrote that despite continuous brushes with the hazards of war and experiences of survival and captivity at the outermost edges of human existence, seafarers' behaviour was mainly determined by the routines of their jobs and their social life. I said, in summary: 'The everyday experience of war was predominantly one of familiar routines within which war was an interruption from outside.' I then illustrated this point at some length by drawing upon entries from Stephen's diary showing that the contemporary landsmen's cliché 'life goes on' applied equally to those tens of thousands of civilian seamen who were so often in the front line of war.

It was the pitch and roll of that diary that finally and decisively shaped my own understanding of the war at sea for the merchant seaman. The diary that has become a book reveals the light and shade of daily life, punctuated by terrifying moments. This was the real stuff of the war at sea and it has been tellingly captured here in this book.

Tony Lane
Professor Emeritus and former Director
of the Seafarers International Research Centre,
University of Cardiff, Wales

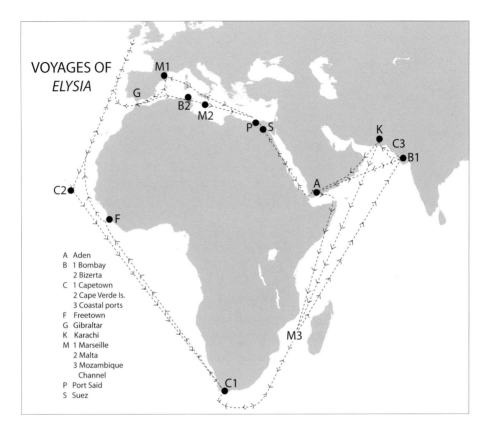

VOYAGES OF *ELYSIA*

A Aden
B 1 Bombay
   2 Bizerta
C 1 Capetown
   2 Cape Verde Is.
   3 Coastal ports
F Freetown
G Gibraltar
K Karachi
M 1 Marseille
   2 Malta
   3 Mozambique
     Channel
P Port Said
S Suez

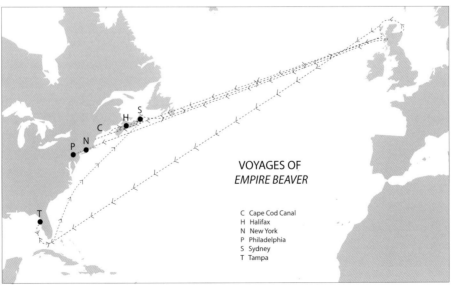

VOYAGES OF *EMPIRE BEAVER*

C Cape Cod Canal
H Halifax
N New York
P Philadelphia
S Sydney
T Tampa

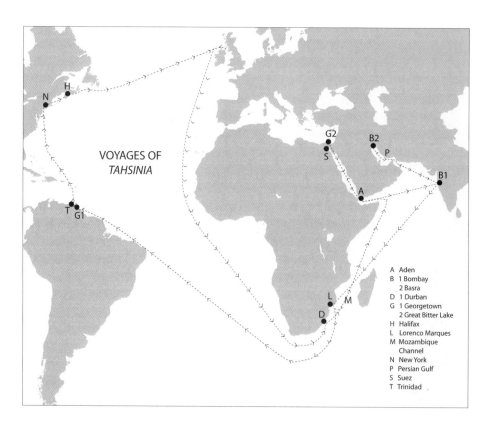

VOYAGES OF
TAHSINIA

A Aden
B 1 Bombay
   2 Basra
D 1 Durban
G 1 Georgetown
   2 Great Bitter Lake
H Halifax
L Lorenco Marques
M Mozambique
   Channel
N New York
P Persian Gulf
S Suez
T Trinidad

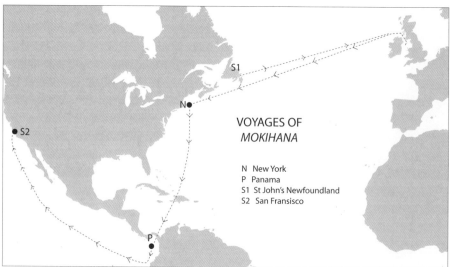

VOYAGES OF
MOKIHANA

N New York
P Panama
S1 St John's Newfoundland
S2 San Fransisco

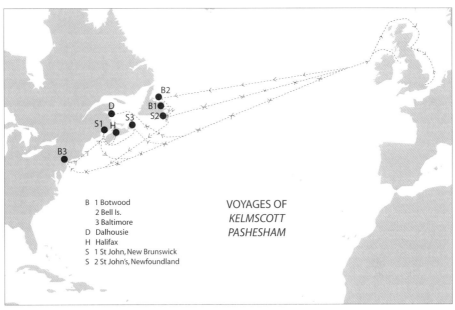

B 1 Botwood
   2 Bell Is.
   3 Baltimore
D Dalhousie
H Halifax
S 1 St John, New Brunswick
S 2 St John's, Newfoundland

VOYAGES OF
KELMSCOTT
PASHESHAM

PORTS VISITED IN
THE BRITISH ISLES

B Barrow in Furness
F Firth of Clyde
G 1 Glasgow
   2 Grangemouth
L 1 London
   2 Liverpool
   3 Loch Ewe
   4 Loch Linnhe
M 1 Manchester
   2 Methil Roads
N Newcastle
S 1 Sunderland
   2 Southampton
   3 Swansea

Western Approaches

CHAPTER 1

Why I became a seaman

I left my Quaker boarding school in England when I was 16 years old. While I was at school my main interests had been sports, music and acting rather than classroom subjects, in which I had not done very well. Like many boys of my age, I had no clear idea of what occupation I should enter. Two that I considered were seafaring and teaching.

Ships and the sea always fascinated me. A childhood friend, George Forrest, was serving his apprenticeship in the deck department of an Anchor Line passenger ship, and I used to visit him when his ship was in Glasgow, Scotland, near my home in Paisley. Seeing his ship and talking with him about what he did made seafaring sound attractive.

Many of my family were teachers, and I discussed entering this profession with my father, who was a scientist and educator. He suggested that I would become a better teacher if I first gained experience in another occupation, away from the confines of a school. He believed this was preferable to going from school to a teacher training college, and then going on to teach in a school. He also wondered whether, with my academic record, I could get into a teachers' college. Having weighed up these considerations I decided to go to sea, keeping in mind that I might later become a teacher. When I told my father of my decision, I reminded him of the advice he had given me.

My father wrote to the Anchor Line about my apprenticing with them, and asked whether I might be better suited as a purser. They replied:

> On the one hand the Purser's duties confine him to a stuffy office where he may have to work for many years before becoming even a Senior Assistant Purser. On the other hand the life of a navigating officer means a life in the open. Certainly there is a four-year apprenticeship to serve, but after that is completed, and providing he passes his examinations, he has every chance of getting a fair salary at an early age.

I decided that life in the open was what I wanted, and after further correspondence and an interview with the company they offered me a position as an apprentice and sent me a copy of the apprenticeship indentures for my father and me to sign. Because the terms of the indenture would largely govern my life for the next four years I will quote from them.

They read, in part

> The said Stephen A. Richardson, with the advice and consent of aforesaid (his father), hereby binds himself to sail in the steamers of the Anchor Line Limited, when and where as required by the Managers of the Company, remaining continuously by the ships as may be required, except when granted leave of absence, for the term of four years from the date of this indenture.

I was to

> faithfully serve any Shipmaster the Company may appoint him to sail with and obey their lawful commands and will not embezzle or waste the company's goods, nor absent himself from their service without leave, nor frequent taverns or alehouses, nor play at unlawful games.

It was not until years later that I noticed the archaic wording of this last sentence in the facsimile of an Elizabethan indenture, and it gave me great pleasure to feel a connection with apprentices who served 400 years before me. I was to take part in a form of traditional training based on learning on the job, through observing masters of the craft and being instructed by them in the skills I would need.

The indenture continues: "In consideration of the premises, the (company) hereby promise and oblige themselves to use all proper means to cause the said Midshipman to be taught the business of a seaman, and the duties of a Navigating Officer... and to pay salary" at the rate of 10 shillings per month (two US dollars at that time), which would increase by annual increments of 10 shillings to £2 a month in the fourth and final year. As a deterrent to my leaving during my apprenticeship, the company required my father to pay them £25 (then $100), returnable to him with interest at the satisfactory completion of my apprenticeship.

The Anchor Line representative, my father and I signed the indenture on 25 August 1937.

CHAPTER 2

Apprenticeship on Elysia

Voyage 1 – August to November 1937

A few days later I was told to join the *Elysia,* docked in Glasgow. She could carry about 150 passengers, had five holds for cargo and made voyages to India. She was built in 1908 with a length of 440 feet and a beam of 53 feet. She was painted in the distinctive colours of the Anchor Line, with a black funnel and hull and white superstructure.

I reported to the Third Mate, who met me at the gangway. He seemed friendly and introduced me to Paddy McClay, my fellow apprentice and cabin mate. Paddy helped me get my gear to our small cabin that was fitted with bunks, a settee, a chest of drawers under the bunks, a hanging locker and a washstand. After we had talked awhile, Paddy took me over to meet McCabe, the Senior Apprentice, who had a tiny cabin of his own opposite ours.

I liked my fellow apprentices. Paddy was small, had a marked Irish accent, loved to talk, seemed full of fun and was about my age. McCabe had nearly finished his apprenticeship, was tall and seemed more reserved and formal. They told me that I would be on watch with the Third Mate, whom I had met, and that I was lucky to be with him. He had recently finished his apprenticeship with the Anchor Line, was understanding, and knew what it was like to be an apprentice. They also told me about our Captain Dunlop, whose early training had been in sailing ships and who felt that apprentices now were pampered and had too easy a life. He had no interest in our training and discouraged the mates from teaching us. They had found that his bark was worse than his bite, however, and that he seemed to go through a cycle of moods. For a while he would occasionally take notice of apprentices, asking them to take messages for him and do odd jobs. Then he would become increasingly grumpy and irritable and seemed to be looking for trouble, until something would trigger off a burst of anger. After that he would become almost pleasant and then the cycle would begin again. They told me that the captain of a ship is often referred to as the "Old Man", although not in his presence.

The loading of the ship resumed after the midday break. The Third Mate put me to work in No. 5 hold, where there was a locker in which was stowed cargo that was liable to be stolen, such as cigarettes and whisky. My job was to see that nothing was stolen or broken by the stevedores who loaded and unloaded ships. Sometimes, to get a drink of whisky, the stevedores would drop a case causing some of the bottles to break, and then hold a container to catch what drained out. Mine was a boring job and not the work I had envisaged, but as I had joined the ship with no previous nautical training I realized that I could only be given unskilled and uninteresting work.

After loading stopped for the day I had tea with my fellow apprentices, and afterwards they told me about the deck department, which was made up of British and Indian members. The British members consisted of the Captain, three mates, four quartermasters, a carpenter and we apprentices. At sea, each apprentice worked two four-hour watches a day: I would be on the 8 to 12 with the Third Mate, Paddy on the 12 to 4 with the Second Mate, and McCabe on the 4 to 8 with the Chief Officer. We were given additional work when off watch. The Indian members were headed by a Serang (a term used by the Indian sailors for Boatswain) and two Tindalls (Assistant Boatswains). They worked under the supervision of the Chief Officer, carried out the maintenance of the ship, stood watches as lookouts, and handled the mooring and tug lines when the ship was entering and leaving port. They lived in quarters at the stern, had their own cooks, practised their own religion and had their own language, and their affairs were governed by the Serang. We each had our own cultures, respected one another's, and only met for work-related activities.

Saying he wanted to show me a memento of the history of the *Elysia*, Paddy took me up to the chartroom located just aft of the bridge. On the wall was a three-foot piece of a torpedo mounted on a plaque. In 1917, during World War I, a torpedo had narrowly missed *Elysia* and this happened again twice. In 1918 she was less lucky, and while in the Mediterranean a torpedo hit her killing 13 people. She managed to limp into Malta where repairs took 10 months. Paddy felt that this piece of torpedo on the wall brought us luck. Then he took me out on the bridge that covered the width of the ship. The central third was an enclosed wheelhouse with windows, where the ship was steered by a quartermaster. On each side of the wheelhouse the bridge was open to the elements. The officer of the watch might stand in the wheelhouse, but we apprentices were to stay outside. If the Captain wanted to stand where we were standing, we were to move to the opposite side. We returned to our cabin, and after I had stowed my gear it was soon time to turn in.

Next morning I returned to my job of preventing pilfering and was glad when the loading of cargo was completed. The entries to the holds were covered with beams and hatch covers. These were then sealed with heavy tarpaulins, secured with steel bars and wedges to protect the holds when heavy seas swept over the decks. I was sent to the bow to watch the Chief Officer supervise the taking in and letting go of the tug and shore lines. The Carpenter operated the windlass used for handling lines and lowering and raising the anchor. The lines from the tugs were made fast aboard, and then the lines securing us to the shore were let go. The tugs pulled us out from the dock and canted us into the river Clyde. Then we let go the tugs and proceeded down stream. We passed the great shipyards, including the one where the first *Queen Mary* was built, and when we came to the wider section of the river the Captain told us to stand down from our "stations". When we reached the mouth of the river, the Pilot climbed down a ladder over the ship's side, transferred to the waiting pilot boat, and we headed for the open sea.

Glasgow to Liverpool

At 8 p.m. I went up to the bridge with Mr MacVicar to keep my first night watch. A fresh southerly wind blew rain into my face, but it was exhilarating and the ship was steady. Mr MacVicar told me to keep a sharp lookout for lights of ships and lighthouses. I remembered Paddy's instructions about where to stand, and when the Captain came out to my side of the bridge I promptly moved across to the other side. We passed Ailsa Craig and the south end of the Isle of Arran. Then in the growing darkness, we steamed south off the Ayrshire coast. Shortly after 10 p.m. Mr MacVicar let me go down to the galley for tea and toast, which tasted marvellous. The watch dragged on for what seemed like an eternity with nothing for me to do except keep a lookout. At midnight when Paddy relieved me for his watch I was very tired, glad to climb into my upper bunk and fall straight to sleep.

Next day when I returned to the bridge at 8 a.m. to relieve McCabe it was still drizzling and visibility was poor. No landmark or lightship had been seen for some time, but by means of the wireless direction finder we found the compass bearing of the Bar Light-ship that marked the entrance to the channel to Liverpool. We sighted the lightship soon afterwards and picked up the Pilot. On the bridge, Mr MacVicar showed me how to enter in a book the time of the Pilot's boarding, the channel markers we passed, and orders to regulate the ship's speed. The purpose of the entries was so that in the event of some mishap leading to an inquiry there would be evidence of the ship's courses and how she had been handled. We followed the buoyed channel, and about half a mile from the Liverpool docks everyone went to "stations": the Second Mate and one apprentice at the stern; the Captain, Third Mate and Senior Apprentice on the bridge; the First Mate, the Carpenter and myself at the bow. By this time it was pouring with rain. The tugs came out and were secured. It took about two and a half hours passing through locks and waiting for bridges to open before we finally reached our dock. We started loading cargo, and again my main job was as policeman down in the locker.

It took two days for the stevedores to load the remaining cargo. Two racehorses were hoisted aboard in their horseboxes and secured on the after deck. We also took on some dogs. I never saw any passengers with the dogs, so assumed they were being sent to owners in India. When the loading finally finished we made ready to go to sea. The passengers embarked, and we had a lifeboat drill in which everyone was mustered at their assigned lifeboat, wearing lifejackets. Some of the lifeboats were swung out. My job was to check that everyone assigned to my lifeboat was present. We also had a fire drill where I had to work an air pump for the man whose job it was, in the event of a fire, to climb down into a hold and put it out.

At 4 p.m. on 4 September we cast off, and it was two and a half hours before we were clear of the docks. A press photographer took photos of *Elysia* as she left, I supposed on the chance that we might get torpedoed off Spain because of their civil war. Those "last boarding" photographs would be easy to sell if something later happened to the *Elysia*.

Liverpool to Marseille

We headed through the buoyed channel, and stood down from our stations. When it was time for me to go on watch at 8 p.m. we were out on the Irish Sea with no land protection from the full force of the wind and seas coming in from the Atlantic. *Elysia* rolled and pitched and I had some difficulty keeping my balance. The weather conditions were deteriorating, and as the hours of keeping a lookout dragged on, I felt increasingly queasy and was sick. At last the end of the watch came and I found release from my misery in sleep.

Next morning the motion of *Elysia* had increased. Before going on watch I began to get to know our dog passengers, who were housed close to my cabin. They seemed to share my misery of feeling seasick, but my seasickness was no excuse for not working. Somehow I got through the watch before being sick over the side. I slept all afternoon and felt terrible during the evening watch. By the following morning the swell had decreased and I felt better. The promenade deck had been empty, but now passengers began to appear to take their morning constitutionals. They soon tired, and drifted off to breakfast and a lazy morning of reclining on deck chairs.

Mr MacVicar gave me what was to become my daily job of marking in chalk the position of the holes for the passengers' nine-hole golf course on the fore deck. The game was played with painted circles of wood that served as balls, and a long handle with one end that fitted round the curve of the ball acting as a golf club. (They were also used in shuffleboard.) I found the marking job tedious, and could not see why the holes had not been marked with paint, thus saving the daily chalking.

In the days that followed, sometimes I would get a break from keeping a lookout and be sent on errands. Mr MacVicar showed me how to read the barometric pressure and the water and air temperature, and how to estimate the direction and force of the wind and sea, read the dial showing the number of nautical miles the ship had travelled and enter the information in the log book. The job I most disliked was "bilges and tanks". Every day the Carpenter dropped a sounding rod into the bilges of each hold to check that no water had entered, because the presence of water might indicate a leak. The Carpenter recorded his measures in pencil in notebooks that became dirty and stained. For official purposes, a neat copy was required. For some reason no copy had been made for over a year and, as junior apprentice, I was given the job, when off watch, of bringing the neat copy up to date. A duller job could not have been conceived of, and I hated the endless hours spent over several months until the copying was finished.

We apprentices were not supposed to speak to passengers, but there was no way that they could be prevented from speaking to us. If we were caught speaking to them, we would claim that the initiative came from the passengers and that it would have been rude of us not to respond. For example, one day I was sitting out on the after deck darning socks when a young woman passenger came to watch what I was doing, and then remarked that she could do a much better job. Another passenger, overhearing, challenged her to show that she was better. By that time several other passengers had gathered round, and I suggested a sock-darning contest. Several agreed to participate, and as I had a number of socks with holes, I helpfully suggested that I would provide the socks. These were distributed to the competitors and next day we gathered with the finished work. One of the stewardesses acted as judge, and wisely decided the result was a draw between a passenger and myself.

At meal times the officers ate with the passengers, but we ate with the children at a separate table and time. I believed that this rule, along with not being allowed to speak to passengers, was to emphasize that we were still in training and held a more childlike status. The mothers who came in to supervise their children ignored us and talked to each other about dieting, their children's ailments and how to keep a permanent wave while at sea.

With the warmer weather arriving as we approached the Straits of Gibraltar, the Captain ordered a change from our blue uniforms to lighter white tropical attire. Once in the Mediterranean we kept a sharp lookout for mines that had broken adrift from minefields, laid along the Spanish coast as the result of their civil war. This had started in 1936 between the incumbent government left wing and the nationalist right wing led by General Franco. It was escalating, with increasing loss of life and reports of brutal mass killings by both sides. Spanish submarines had attacked neutral merchant ships, so to avoid attack we kept well clear of the Spanish coast. Several times we had to alter course suddenly to avoid a floating object that looked like a floating mine but turned out to be a box or some such object.

The Captain disliked any unnecessary talk between mates and apprentices when on watch, but when he was not around Mr MacVicar and I enjoyed talking and getting to know each other. In appearance he was good-looking, well built, of medium height, and well coordinated. He wore his uniform cap tilted back, suggesting an air of informality. The Captain also disliked officers smoking on watch, so to avoid being caught Mr MacVicar held his cigarette with the lighted end held concealed in the palm of his hand. His only unusual feature was his sunken cheeks, which were due, as I later learned, to his having had all his teeth pulled out and replaced with false teeth in order to avoid the pains of toothache at sea, where no dentist was available. Brought up in a large family in a small town on the coast of Scotland, Mr MacVicar and his siblings were good students and athletes. Their father was a Presbyterian minister with high standards of conduct who could be strict with his children. Their mother was more easygoing, loved parties, and helped in the church. Mr MacVicar had a wide range of interests and a good sense of humour, so when we talked the watches passed more quickly.

In reply to Mr MacVicar's inquiries about my background, I told him that my brother, sister and I had all been adopted and had been fortunate in having such good adoptive parents. Our father was a scientist, a member of the Royal Society, who had an innovative, enquiring mind and a lively sense of humour. He never talked down to us, was a good listener and freely shared ideas with us. As a Quaker he was a conscientious objector who twice resigned from jobs that were taken over by the military. During World War I he had joined the Friends (Quaker) Ambulance Unit in France, taking wounded men away from the front lines. My mother, a former teacher, did volunteer work at boys' clubs, often read aloud to us, took us to the theatre, and encouraged us to be independent and to develop our interests. With both parents we would go camping and for walks in the country. At meals there were often wide-ranging discussions of ideas and current affairs. We lived in London and later moved to Paisley, Scotland.

As *Elysia* headed north for Marseille, the warm, calm conditions in the Mediterranean changed rapidly owing to the mistral, a gale force cold wind that came down from the Alps. The ship responded to the mounting seas by pitching heavily and slowing from thirteen to five knots, and for a period to less than one knot. Occasionally a particularly heavy sea broke over the bow and swept down the fore deck, with spray coming right over the bridge. The motion of the ship made the dogs miserable. They were frightened by the ship's movement and the noise of the alternate racing and straining of the engine as the propeller rose and fell from the sea. Because there was a chance of the dogs being washed overboard, we moved them from the after deck into the alleyway near our cabin. The horses could not be moved, but they were enclosed in their horseboxes securely lashed to the deck. Next morning I knew the storm was over when

I woke to hear the steady beat of the engine and found the sea a great deal calmer as we sighted the French coast. By afternoon we had docked at Marseille, over a day late because of the storm. We took on water, some passengers, cars, and three racehorses accompanied by a groom. We sailed on 14 September.

Marseille to Port Said

Our route took us through the Straits of Bonifacio, which separate Corsica from Sardinia. The scenery on the islands was wild and rugged, and the mountains looked so much like fortresses that it was hard to distinguish rocks from castles. We passed the island of Stromboli, one of the most active volcanoes in the world, and then went on through the Italian Strait of Messina. On the main building in the town of Messina was written in huge letters "DUCE", for the Italian leader, Mussolini. It was tantalizing to be so near such beautiful places and not to be able to go ashore and explore.

Every day shortly before noon the Captain, mates and we apprentices gathered on the bridge and it became a place of hurry and mild excitement. The Captain and the mates got out their sextants, Paddy stood by the clock and engine room telegraph, and I stood by the log that recorded our mileage. At noon the Captain and mates measured the angle of the sun above the horizon, Paddy rang the engine room telegraph and eight bells on the ship's bell, and I recorded the day's mileage from the dial of the log and reset it to zero. The Old Man and the mates then retired to the chart room to work out the noon position and compare their results. McCabe then filled in the particulars of the day's run and the position of the ship and posted the information for the passengers.

There were two weekly functions that we apprentices had to attend. On Sundays at 10.30 a.m. we had inspection, when the ship's company mustered and the Captain, Chief Officer, the doctor and the ship's Butler inspected the accommodations and then the crew. All the officers not on duty and we apprentices stood in line wearing our uniforms. The Indian sailors turned out in their dress uniform: a white blouse, silk socks, and a red scarf wrapped round their fezzes. The Serang and the two Tindalls wore silver chains with a bosun's whistles attached. After this ceremony, at 11 a.m., we would attend the church service held for the passengers, who were summoned by the ringing of the ship's bell. The service was conducted by a travelling minister, a passenger who volunteered or the Captain.

Twice a week we apprentices were responsible for "baggage days", when the passengers could get their baggage from the hold where it was stowed and take out what they wanted. McCabe stood on deck above the open hatch, and found out what the passengers wanted. He then gave the name and the description of the trunk to Paddy and me down in the hold and we found whatever the passenger wanted. Two of the sailors tied the baggage on a rope and others heaved it up on deck. Sometimes there were incidents that enlivened the proceedings. A lady found she had locked her trunk with the key inside. The Carpenter was called to break open the trunk, and afterwards had to mend it. Another lady wanted something out of one of her trunks and did not know in which one it was, so we had to bring up all of her six trunks. One passenger found some moths in a bedding roll. The moths had also found homes in other baggage and were flying in swarms, getting into our shirts and hair. The Old Man and the Chief Officer came along to see about it and finally decided to move any baggage that moths might enter into an unused cabin.

We had little leisure time after eight hours on watch and another two hours of job assignments. Since no entertainment was provided for us, we were thrown on our own resources. I read a lot, especially during rough weather, and wrote letters and my diary. I was restricted in the number of people I could socialize with, and conversed mainly with my fellow apprentices. Between six and eight in the evening I would often join the Third Mate, the junior engineers and the Wireless Operator on the after deck where we customarily met. Another place I sometimes visited was the cabin of the two middle-aged Scottish stewardesses who always enjoyed a talk.

We had good weather on this passage, which made it easier to provide entertainment for the passengers. During the day, deck golf and tennis were popular. (Instead of using a tennis racket and ball, a rope quoit was thrown and caught by hand.) One evening there was a scavenger hunt, with passengers rushing around looking for a list of things, such as a 1917 penny and a tram ticket. Another evening there was a dance on the promenade deck with music provided by gramophone records. The deck was draped with flags and fairy lights, and when not dancing the passengers behaved like children larking about. Refreshments were served, so at the end of our watch I plundered the galley for leftover sandwiches and ice cream, which I shared with the Third Mate and the Fourth Mate at our customary midnight supper.

As we approached Egypt, the Nile showed its influence by changing the colour of the sea from blue to green. We sighted the Port Said light at 5 p.m. on 18 September, but it was dark by the time we were tied up and the passengers had gone ashore. The town was brightly lit and fishing dhows were sailing out of the harbour. The waterfront was lined with trees, people were laughing and singing, and swarms of boats rushed about in great excitement, without any obvious purpose. I was on cargo work until midnight and felt that we were really getting into the East, which until then I had only read about.

Port Said to Bombay

We only stayed at Port Said overnight in order to take on water, oil and supplies. I was wakened at 4 a.m. for stations and went up on the bridge. The Pilot came aboard; we slipped our moorings and headed inland into the Suez Canal. I remained on the bridge until 7 a.m., when I was relieved for breakfast. By then we were in the Canal, with salt marshes on both sides. Along the Canal there was a road and railway that ran from Port Said to Suez. Soon desert took over from the salt marshes, but every few miles we would pass a "station", a small group of huts and bungalows from which officials regulated the Canal traffic. Ships were not allowed to pass each other unless one was moored to the bank. We had to tie up twice, and had boring waits while ships passed us at half-mile intervals. We passed a railway station with a sign "TRAINS FOR CAIRO, CALAIS, LONDON". At the same place was a large herd of resting camels.

During my evening watch we were going through one of the lakes that formed part of the Canal. All ships had searchlights rigged on their bows. We could see these lights reflected in the sky before the ships came over the horizon. At intervals across the lake there were buoys with different coloured flashing lights marking the channel. Just before midnight we reached Suez and, you will believe me, I was glad to get to bed.

The heat struck us as soon as we started on our passage through the Red Sea. On the second day it became hotter than I had ever experienced, with the temperature at noon 100 degrees Fahrenheit in the shade. The air was still, because the breeze made by the speed of the ship was exactly counteracted by the following wind. It was even hotter in the engine room with the added heat from the boilers. The engine room staff really suffered. I got patches of prickly heat, a red skin rash that felt itchy and burning, but it was nothing compared to what some of the engineers experienced.

The cabins were so hot that at night many of the passengers slept out on deck on mattresses, and when I went on errands from the bridge I had to be careful not to trip over sleeping bodies. To alleviate the heat, the sailors rigged awnings to shade the open decks and put up a small swimming pool made of canvas and wood. When no one was around I would go for a swim, and though the water temperature was 90 degrees Fahrenheit and so salty that it stung my eyes, I enjoyed the exercise. On our third day in the Red Sea, we had welcome relief from the worst of the heat when the wind swung round from north to south, and added to rather than subtracted from the breeze made by the ship. At last we passed out of the Red Sea through the Straits of Hormuz and entered the Gulf of Aden.

On 24 September we arrived at Aden and moored to buoys in the harbour. Oil and water pipelines were brought aboard and we spent the night working cargo. Swarms of small boats came alongside carrying merchants hoping to sell our passengers goods such as cigarettes and silk clothing. They carried on their trade by throwing lines up to the passengers with an accuracy that would put a cricketer to shame. Attached to the line would be a basket, and after the passenger and boatman merchant had agreed on a price the boatman would put the article in the basket and the passenger would pull it up, put the money in the basket and lower it back down. The noise of the haggling for price was almost deafening. I bought a silk scarf and had my first experience of bargaining for the price, which was great fun. Finally I got to bed at 2 a.m., but not to sleep, because of the noise.

We were on our way again for the five-day crossing of the Arabian Sea. When I was called to go on watch the sea was calm and there was a pleasant breeze. The weather at this time of year was the best for crossing to Bombay, in contrast to the monsoon season, when the sea was rough and the weather was hot and humid. Mr MacVicar told me this was the time for the annual "fishing fleet", when young single women went to India from Britain in search of husbands. The fishing was good because there were so many single men from Britain in the Indian Civil Service and other administrative jobs. The unsuccessful women generally returned to Britain before the next monsoon arrived.

John, the Fourth Engineer, enjoyed going to dances at the Seaman's Mission in Bombay. I didn't know how to dance and wanted to learn, so John, who was a good dancer, offered to give me lessons. We practised daily out on deck, with John taking the part of the female dancer and leading me through the steps of the waltz and the foxtrot. He was very encouraging, and by the time we reached Bombay I was, he said, ready for the Mission dances

On the evening watch as we approached Bombay, we could smell the rich, thick smell of the land. The passengers were larking about, as it was their last night aboard. Even the Captain and the Chief Officer, generally so solemn and dignified, were firing water pistols from the after end of the bridge at passengers passing beneath them on the promenade deck. A little before 10 p.m. we sighted the lights of Bombay reflected in the sky, and just before the end of the watch two lights became visible from the lighthouses at the entrance to the harbour.

At Bombay

Late on 1 October we anchored in Bombay harbour until daylight, when we were called to stations. We were rewarded with a glorious sunrise. We weighed anchor and the Pilot took us to Ballard Pier where the passengers disembarked along with their baggage. The policemen at the pier wore quaint uniforms: yellow flat hat, blue jacket suit with yellow facings, short blue "plus fours" with bare legs, a truncheon, and an umbrella carried like a rifle. After the passengers had left, we were again called to "stations" and moved into the Alexandra Dock. There we discharged and later loaded cargo. I was put on the day shift. The first few hours were fun as we were unloading cars and I steered them in the hold while they were being pushed on to slings to lift them ashore. There were some Baby Austins I had difficulty with because I am over six feet tall and my legs were jammed against the steering wheel. Later my job was to go round the hatches noting breakages. When I climbed down into the holds, the rungs of the ladder were so heated by the sun that I got my hands slightly burned. The stevedores were Pathans from the north-west frontier of India. I had been told that they took this work in order to save up enough money to buy a rifle and then return to the frontier to shoot British soldiers. They were tall, powerful men with long black beards, and wore turbans and what looked like long-sleeved nightshirts. While we had no common language, I enjoyed being with them and sensed that they were friendly.

I had been aboard *Elysia* for four weeks, so it was good to get ashore for a walk. Eager to try out the steps I had learned from my dancing lessons, I went with several of the crew to a dance at the Seaman's Mission. Unfortunately it was difficult to find a partner since there were a great many ships in port and the men outnumbered the girls by four to one.

Another evening several of us went to the pictures, and since they ended before 9 p.m. we decided to go for a walk around town. We left the broad, well-lit streets and entered the narrow alleys of the Old Town. On each side were small open shops with the owners sitting cross-legged amidst their wares. A customer would approach and soon there would be a vigorous argument before an agreement on price was reached. The smell of sandalwood incense hung heavily in the air. Beggars lay asleep on the pavements and an occasional rat scampered across the narrow street. People of all shades of brown, and different dress, height and figure, walked or shuffled along the streets, while a few dogs sniffed round the gutters looking for food. The whole scene was strange, new, and fascinating to me. After passing through several of these streets, we suddenly came out on a main avenue. It seemed like stepping back into a London street.

After the discharging of cargo from a hold was finished, the stevedores cleaned it. Then the loading started and I was given the job of seeing that plenty of dunnage mats were put between the bags being loaded and the steel plates. Without the mats the moisture condensing on the hot hull plates would make the bags damp and spoil the contents.

Paddy had been working the day shift while I had been on the night shift. On the day we swapped shifts we were given an afternoon off. It was our only chance to go to a swimming place, Breach Candy, and the Chief Officer gave us five rupees for our expenses, which was very good of him. We left after lunch and took a taxi that cost about two shillings (20 cents) for three to four miles. Breach Candy had an indoor and an outdoor pool. The indoor one was for diving and swimming laps. The outdoor one was like a small lake and had diving boards, rafts and water chutes, and was surrounded by lawns with palm trees. We had a marvellous afternoon, diving, swimming and lazing in the sun, and then sat down at tables where we had tea under the palm trees. To prevent birds swooping down and stealing our sandwiches, boys walked around waving large fans on poles. We got back to *Elysia* just in time to start night work. It had begun to rain, and since only manganese ore could be loaded during rain there was nothing for us to watch. We were told that we could knock off. This was great news. We were so high-spirited that we tidied up the cabin before turning in.

Bombay to Karachi via coastal ports

Having finished loading after a five-day stay in Bombay we sailed on 5 October. Since joining *Elysia*, all my time and energy had been absorbed by getting used to life at sea, and the work that I had been given. Now I felt it was time to begin studying the four-year correspondence course set up by the Glasgow Technical College. The purpose of the course was to prepare apprentices for the Second Mate Certificate examinations given by the Board of Trade at the completion of the apprenticeship. If I passed I would then be eligible to sail as a Third Mate or Second Mate in charge of a watch at sea. The syllabus covered the knowledge I would probably not acquire in my work as an apprentice. It would be up to me to carry out the coursework because I would receive no supervision from the ship's officers. My only companions while studying were large cockroaches that were as common as flies. When I was at school I had dissected cockroaches and given a paper on them to the Natural History Society, so they did not bother me and I became quite fond of them.

During an evening watch, the Chief Officer asked me round to his cabin at the after end of the bridge to listen on the radio to Big Ben striking 4 p.m. in London. It was about 9.30 p.m. our time and it was a strange feeling to hear Big Ben so far away. We were coasting along the northern shore of the Gulf of Cambay. The coastline consisted mainly of sand or low cliffs with an occasional patch of trees and grass. At intervals there were small settlements with buoys anchored offshore. During one afternoon we took on a pilot and reached our first stop, Bhavnaga, a small town where we lay at anchor offshore for the next two days loading cotton, oilcake and groundnuts. The water was muddy brown and the powerful tidal currents reached eight knots at half tide. Tugs brought out the barges with the cargo we were to load. Because of the power of the current, the tugs had great difficulty in getting the barges alongside.

Next morning my job was to see that the cargo was properly stowed, but as the stevedores were doing a good job there was very little to do except take an occasional look round. When I came on watch at 8 p.m. the ship had taken on a new appearance in the dark. Arc lamps threw wide circles of light on the hatches, the barges and the rapidly moving muddy water. Native cooks squatted on the barges over small wood fires preparing food for the stevedores who worked 20 hours a day until the loading was completed. Above the noise of the winches we heard the cries of "Avis" and "Aria"(up and down) as men directed the winch operators, and the sound of the hoots of the tugs bringing out the lighters. Round the lights was a myriad of insects of curious shapes and colours.

On the passage to our next port, Navalaki, I woke to hear the ship's siren give a blast every second minute, telling me we were in fog. When I went up on the bridge for the morning watch, the fog was thick. The ship was moving ahead slowly. The only sounds were the monotonous wail of our siren and the muffled breaking of small wavelets from the ship's bow. Everything was damp, and although the temperature was high, the fog was cold and clammy as it groped its way into every crack and cranny. On the bridge, the Captain, Chief Officer and Third Mate stood silently peering into the fog, and we strained to hear an answering fog signal from another ship that might be approaching, Every now and again we heard the dull whirr of our sounding machine as the Second Mate checked to make sure we were in deep water. The machine lowered a weighted container at the end of a wire containing a glass tube filled with coloured liquid that showed the depth.

After what seemed hours the fog rolled away. There was an almost audible sigh, and tense figures relaxed after the strain of the past hours. The experience was enough to instil in me the seaman's fear of fog, and I understood why a mariner prefers storms. We spent a long time determining our position, finally finding that we were at the entrance to the Gulf of Cutch, but too far north because of a current we had not anticipated. We then set our course for Navalaki, where we loaded more cargo.

At our next port, Port Okha, Mr MacVicar and I went round the holds to measure how much space was left for Karachi cargo. The holds were like a Turkish bath, with the sun beating down on them all day. Mr MacVicar had a narrow escape when the stevedores were uncovering part of a hold that we were in. They let a hatch cover slip. It bounced off a girder, and fell and grazed MacVicar's arm. Luckily I had yelled a warning to him and he had jumped behind the ladder. The Chief Officer saw the incident and gave the stevedore foreman a thorough ticking off.

We were all glad to get finished with the coastal ports and reach Karachi on 12 October. During our two-day stay we were docked at Kinan, a few miles away from Karachi. We completed loading cargo with bales of cotton and groundnuts. Chips (the Carpenter) and I walked to the nearby village of Karmari to look at the shops. Returning we saw some camel carts, with the camels padding along with great strides, and just behind an ox cart, with the oxen taking three steps to every one of the camel. We saw some cows eating fruit from a stall, with the stall keeper making no effort to stop them. Hindus revere cows as a symbol of the sanctity of life and of the earth, and allow them to wander freely without interference.

When we were ready to sail, the holds were full of cargo except for spaces for ropes and passengers' luggage. With passengers boarding, stalls appeared on the quay. A snake charmer gave a demonstration with cobras and a mongoose, and local boys were diving for coins. At noon there was a medical examination of the whole ship's company. It was a complete farce, as the doctor came round and merely touched everyone's wrists.

The Elysia – *leaving dock at Glasgow.*

left: *The author on the* Elysia

below: *The wheelhouse Quartermaster steering*

Mr MacVicar taking a shore compass bearing

Serang and sailors watching a haircut

Sunday inspection

Pathans discharging chlorine drums, Bombay

Karachi – off on a picnic on sailing dhow

Camel cart in Karachi

Homeward bound – 15 October to 11 November 1937

[From day to day there was a great deal of repetition in the life of the ship. To spare the reader much of this repetition I will only include from the diary events not already described.]

After leaving Karachi we returned to Bombay to pick up additional passengers, then sailed for Aden and Suez. Part of our cargo was oilcake that was liable to go on fire if the hold temperature became too hot. To monitor the temperature we apprentices, while on watch, went to the ventilators of each hold and lowered a thermometer down to take the hold temperature. An abnormally high temperature would indicate danger of fire. To maximize the circulation of air in the holds we faced one ventilator into the wind and its companion away. Taking the hold temperature of No. 1 hold in rough weather without getting soaked by a wave was an interesting challenge. I waited until after we shipped a sea, and then ran, as fast as the movements of the ship would allow, along the fore deck and up onto the forecastle where the ventilators were situated. Returning I followed the same procedure and generally got back dry.

One evening while going on watch, I passed a rather untidy curly haired man I had not seen before. Later the Second Wireless Operator came up in great excitement and told me he had been standing on the boat deck when a man came up to him and said, "I am a stowaway. Can you get me something to eat?" The man I had seen earlier had hidden in the lifeboat near where the Wireless Operator worked, He would have had to work his passage to Suez, and if he were an army deserter would be put ashore and sent back to India. If not, we would have had to take him to Liverpool and hand him over to the police. The Captain and the ship's officers could get into trouble because they should have searched the ship for stowaways before leaving Bombay.

A few evenings later I was on watch talking with Mr MacVicar when the bell rang from the wireless room and, as usual, I went to fetch the message. I was told to take it immediately to the Captain, who was watching a game of draughts. He took the cablegram to read in the chartroom, then came out and told me to get the doctor at once. The doctor came and conferred with the Captain, after which I was sent along to the radio room with a message to dispatch. Several messages came and went during the next half hour, and then the Old Man and the doctor left the bridge. Because all the messages were clipped together in the chart room, I soon learned what had been happening. A Chinese sailor on a nearby ship was seriously ill and the ship had no doctor. (Only passenger ships were required to carry a doctor.) His captain sent the details of the case by radio for our doctor to diagnose and prescribe treatment. We later learned that the sailor had recovered, so the use of wireless probably saved his life.

A great many birds landed on the ship while we were in the Mediterranean and we watched them being stalked by the ship's cat. The birds seemed to make a fool of the cat on purpose. When the cat had nearly caught an unsuspecting bird, another bird would fly low, distracting its attention and enabling the first bird to escape. Later on I found a small bird lying on the galley deck. When it tried to fly, it hit a bulwark and fell back. I picked it up and took it up to the bridge. Because the Old Man was there I had to wait until he left, and then I asked Mr MacVicar what to do with the bird. He suggested that I make a nest of cushions on the settee in his cabin, put some milk and breadcrumbs near by and leave the bird in the nest. I did this, and after our watch we took the bird out on deck and it flew away.

Shortly after arriving at Marseille, the Anchor Line passenger ship *Circassia*, on her maiden voyage to India, docked near us. A large crowd had already gathered on the dock, and all our crew who could get away went over to see her. Our ship's doctor, Paddy and I, who were in uniform, went to the gangway of the *Circassia* where everyone except journalists was being held back. When the gendarmes saw us coming they opened a lane for us, and to our vast amusement, saluted and let us go on board. We acted the part, giving the gendarmes a curt nod, and walked up the gangway as if we owned the ship. When we got on board the passengers, who were all being kept back, made a lane for us and we stalked through. Our Old Man, who was on the quay with the Third Mate, exclaimed, "Look at those bloody apprentices, they have gone to take charge already."

We met one of the *Circassia's* apprentices and, although we had never met before, greeted each other like long lost friends. He took us to his cabin, which he shared with another apprentice. It was palatial compared to ours. We were introduced to the other apprentices and chatted a while, before Paddy and I went to explore the ship. When we found the gym, we had great fun trying out the mechanical horse, the bicycles, the rowing machine and other devices. I was riding the horse side-saddle with the beast at full gallop and Paddy was on the sculling machine when our Old Man walked in. We did not know what he would say, so beat a retreat in as dignified a manner as possible. Whenever we met any of their crew, they came over and shook hands and had a chat. The meeting of the two crews was like a school reunion with everyone in the best of spirits. We noticed that "birds of a feather flock together", or rather that the doctors immediately got together, the various officers, the engineers and so on, all the best of friends. We returned to *Elysia,* and when the loading was completed we left Marseille.

We anchored briefly at Gibraltar to discharge and load cargo and saw many British and American warships lying in the harbour. Shortly after we sailed, a Spanish warship circled round us with her searchlight playing on us, rather like a little dog smelling a big one. Why she did it we could only guess. We had surprisingly good weather during our passage through the Bay of Biscay, but as we approached England it turned so cold that during an evening watch Mr MacVicar said I could come inside the wheelhouse as long as the Old Man did not see me.

We reached Liverpool on 18 November, where we discharged part of our cargo, then left the docks bound for the entrance of the Manchester ship canal. A high wind was blowing, making the ship very difficult to manoeuvre. At the lock marking the entrance to the canal, a tug was pulling us towards the windward side to prevent *Elysia* from being driven onto the lee shore by the wind. The towing line suddenly broke and we had an exciting time until we got a new towrope fastened aboard. During the night while we were tied up at the side of the canal the wind dropped, and we started along the canal at 5 a.m. At intervals we would enter a lock and stop. The lock gates would close and the water would rise to the next level of the canal. Then the upper gate of the lock would open and we would proceed. We reached the Manchester docks in the afternoon, and as soon as I was free I lay down on the settee and slept like a log until teatime, having had little sleep for the past 24 hours. After three days we returned along the canal and had an uneventful passage to our homeport of Glasgow. There I was given a few days' leave and found my time at sea had heightened my appreciation of being at home.

My father asked whether I preferred being at sea to being at school. I replied that I would rather be at school where I had wonderful experiences participating in sports and physical activities, music, and drama. Also I had the intellectual stimulation of good teachers, and many good friends. I had mixed feelings about going to sea. It fulfilled some of my expectations in enabling me to experience the sea in its various moods, see places I otherwise would never have seen, and feel pride in being part of the ship's company. What I disliked was how much of my work was spent in what I would call "attentive inactivity". For example, the long hours of keeping a lookout when on watch; standing around at "stations" entering and leaving port; and keeping anchor watches where there was little to do beyond checking that the anchor was not dragging. I had a tendency to daydream, or get lost in some line of thought, and I was not good at doing nothing intelligently. Although my indentures read that I was to be taught "the business of a seaman, and the duties of a navigating officer", apart from the time I spent with Mr MacVicar I had been given no formal instruction and most of my jobs when off watch taught me little.

One thing was clear. I was determined to finish my apprenticeship, and get back the £25 deposit the company had required my father to pay. I was also too proud to give up what I had started.

Voyages 2 and 3 – December 1937 to May 1938

On the next two voyages on *Elysia*, I continued to be on watch with Mr MacVicar and to do the same sort of things. But I was becoming more accustomed to what had earlier seemed hard, and was beginning to become more useful in my work.

Despite having to instruct me surreptitiously because of Captain Dunlop's attitude towards apprentices, Mr MacVicar taught me such things as how to take compass bearings of shore objects and lay them off on the chart in order to find the ship's position; how to use the wireless direction finder; and how to steer the ship. The more I learned and was able to do, the more interesting watchkeeping became. Now that Mr MacVicar knew me better he was more comfortable in leaving me on the bridge while he went into the chartroom to work out the ship's position. I was careful to maintain the proper relationship of an apprentice to a Third Mate, but outside of our work we were becoming good friends. On warm and sunny afternoons Mr MacVicar and I, and sometimes others, would sunbathe up on the boat deck that was out of bounds for the passengers. We used to talk, read and write letters, and I would sometimes study assignments for my correspondence course.

An important skill we apprentices had to master was signalling by Morse, semaphore, and the international code of flag signals used to exchange information with other ships. First we had to master the letters of the alphabet for each form of signalling and gain the manual skills needed to send and receive messages. To make up a flag signal we practised selecting the needed flags, putting them in their correct sequence, clipping them together and finally hoisting the signal. We took pride in the speed and accuracy that we achieved. Sometimes the Third Mate would test our progress in Morse and semaphore. One of the rare occasions when the Captain complimented us was for our flag signalling, because good signalling indicated a smart ship and reflected well on him.

On this passage to India we had only one passenger. This made our lives more enjoyable, as we had the run of the ship, and could dress more casually and take over the recreation facilities that the passengers generally used. We organized tournaments in deck tennis and golf, used the promenade deck as a running track, and when the weather was hot were free to use the swimming pool at any time. I loved the opportunities to get exercise.

Weather conditions in the Arabian Sea and at the Indian ports were hot and humid. At Bombay I had the choice of sleeping in an unpleasantly hot cabin, or out on deck where I was at the mercy of mosquitoes. I was glad to get back to sea and escape the mosquitoes and sweltering heat.

The passengers were always a source of interest, and on the homeward passage we had more of them. With so little out of the ordinary going on at sea, Mr MacVicar and I devised a novel form of entertainment. We would select a woman passenger and ask everyone in the crew with whom she had some contact to observe her carefully for a 24-hour period. They would then report to us what they had learned. We found that some women were thought by the senior officers to be charming and interesting, but the same women treated their stewardesses like dirt, and ordered them around. We wondered whether they treated their Indian servants in the same way. Other women were reported by all to be kind, considerate and courteous.

The possessions I most missed having on the ship were my two clarinets, which had different pitches (A and B flat). I had started learning to play the clarinet at school, where I had lessons, and progressed to playing both in the school orchestra and a town orchestra. Uncertain whether I would be allowed to play on *Elysia,* I had left them at home. I hated to lose what skill I had acquired, and playing gave me great pleasure, so I decided to bring them with me on my next voyage.

Although our world was largely restricted by the confines of the ship, the wireless reports we received and what we learned in port indicated an increasingly troubled and unsettled Europe. The Spanish civil war between the incumbent left-wing government and the Nationalist right wing led by General Franco was escalating. Germany was speeding up her rate of rearmament and, in response, Britain and France were following suit. On board I was beginning to hear talk about the likelihood of war. On my third voyage, just as we were leaving Liverpool, we read the disturbing news that German troops had invaded Austria without encountering any resistance, and Germany had declared a German–Austrian alliance.

Voyage 4 – June to August 1938

When I returned to the ship after a short leave I found a number of changes in the crew. Captain Dunlop, the Chief Officer, Mr MacVicar and McCabe, the Senior Apprentice, had been transferred to other Anchor Line ships. They were replaced by Captain Johnson, Mr McGilvray, the Chief Officer, a Third Mate and Cowie, an apprentice. Cowie being junior to me in sea time, I moved to the 12 to 4 watch with Mr Lieper, the new Second Mate, and Paddy became the Senior Apprentice. My sleep was now broken into two parts, as I had to wake up in time to go on watch at midnight and go back to sleep when the watch ended at 4 a.m. Surprisingly, I found this watch less tiring than the 8 to 12 and it gave me more free time.

Mr Lieper, with whom I now shared a watch, had prime responsibility for matters related to navigation, and I helped him in his work. He showed me how to organize charts so that those needed were readily available in the chart drawers. To keep the charts up to date he used "Notices to Mariners", published at regular intervals by the Admiralty and listing all the worldwide changes of buoys, lights and wrecks. We used this source to make the needed changes on our charts, an essential but time-consuming and boring job. Besides this Mr Lieper introduced me to the use of the sextant to measure the angle of stars and the sun above the horizon, and taught me to take the exact time from the chronometer. From this information he showed me how to work out the ship's position. When at "stations" entering and leaving port my place was now at the stern, sending and receiving information by telephone between the bridge and Mr Lieper. Much of the time there was nothing for me to do but watch and learn from what the Second Mate did. I got along well with Mr Lieper, but we never developed the kind of friendship I had had with Mr MacVicar.

The new Captain and officers made a big difference in our lives as apprentices. They encouraged and helped us to learn new skills – a refreshing change from Captain Dunlop. We were expected to work two hours a day in addition to our watches, and now we were given tasks that would teach us skills of practical seamanship. These included splicing ropes and wire hawsers, checking to see that all the gear in the lifeboats was in good order, scraping rust from decks and bulkheads and painting the cleaned surface, learning to sew canvas to make covers or repair awnings, and repairing torn flags. Captain Johnson would sometimes question us apprentices about our work.

I was able to play my clarinets in the cabin I shared with Cowie because it did not seem to disturb anyone else. I chose times when Cowie was on watch. To my surprise and delight I found that Cowie had brought with him a piano accordion, which he let me use. I could play a piano by ear so could use the keyboard, and I started to learn the chords provided by the buttons on the accordion.

I had my first experience of the annual monsoon on our passage from Aden to Bombay. The sea was rough with a heavy swell. At times the wind reached gale force. The fore deck was often awash, and at night the seas breaking over the forecastle were lit with the cold light of phosphorescence. We had to keep our porthole closed to prevent seas pouring in. Without ventilation and with the heat and humidity the cabin was like a Turkish bath, and to add to the discomfort I was seasick.

While we were at Bombay, cargo work frequently had to stop owing to downpours of rain. The monsoon broke the intense heat we had felt on the previous voyage, but the rain and high humidity discouraged us from going ashore. The weather wore on our nerves and we became irritable and short tempered. The return passage across the Arabian Sea was even more unpleasant as we headed into the wind and seas. My eyes began to trouble me, and reading and writing only made them worse. Playing the clarinet and accordion and sleeping was all I could do. After a few days my eyes became so painful that it was torture to go into strong light, so the Chief Officer put me on night watches from 8 p.m. to 4 a.m. As the eye condition slowly cleared up, I was able to return to my 12 to 4 watch. As we finally left the monsoon and then the heat of the Red Sea, the cool, dry weather of the Mediterranean had a tonic effect on us and our spirits rose.

When we reached Liverpool in August, preparations for war were evident. Guns had been placed on top of the warehouses along the docks and soldiers were standing at the locks as we were passed through. The Chief Engineer told me he had been given orders to take on extra oil fuel, in case war was declared and we had to go round

Africa instead of through the Mediterranean. It was expected that Italy would side with Germany, and if she did she could easily blockade the passage of ships passing through the Mediterranean.

Voyage 5 – September to November 1938

Paddy left, so I became Senior Apprentice and moved to the 4 to 8 watch with Mr McGilvray, the Chief Officer, whom we called Dougie when not in his presence. He had the lilting speech of a Highlander and was taciturn in manner. In appearance he was heavily built, had a ruddy complexion, and his uniform was somewhat dowdy. My station now was on the forecastle with Dougie and the Carpenter, so I learned what they did by watching them.

When I found that Dougie had trouble hearing orders from the bridge I would repeat them to him. Shortly after leaving England we learned by wireless that the Prime Minister, Neville Chamberlain, had signed a non-aggression pact with Germany, Italy and France, and declared that it brought "peace in our time". This good news meant that we could still go through the Mediterranean.

The 4 to 8 watch was by far the most interesting because dawn and dusk were the two best times for establishing the ship's position by using star sights. I noticed that Dougie was having difficulty seeing the stars. He wanted me to take the star sights and work out our position, and became increasingly dependent on me to obtain the ship's position. He also had difficulty in seeing the lighthouses and other landmarks we used in coastal navigation, so I gradually took over this task for him as well. As a result, I had an unusual opportunity to develop and practise navigational skills. On one occasion I made a careless mistake in working out our position and gave it to Dougie. He then gave it to the Old Man, who altered course and soon found the position given him was incorrect. Dougie told the Old Man that he had made the mistake and accepted the blame. The following morning I expected Dougie to bawl me out, but instead he allowed me to take sights as usual and accepted my position as if I had never made a mistake. I thought it exceedingly good of him and took the greatest care after that not to make a mistake. In addition to watchkeeping, Dougie was responsible for the work of the Indian sailors in the maintenance of the ship. With his long sea service he had become very good at working with the Serang, and the sailors and I learned by being with him.

Dougie was a very complex person. When we were on watch and not busy I tried to get him to talk in order to pass the time, but found the only topic on which he would converse was religion, where he held fundamentalist views. When I tried to edge him away from religion to get him to talk about himself, he would quickly revert to silence. When the swimming pool was rigged on the fore deck we could look down on it from the bridge and watch the swimmers and those sitting by the pool. When a nubile, attractive young woman wearing a scanty bathing costume made an appearance, Dougie would look down at her spellbound and expostulate in his broad Highland accent, "That's terrible. It shouldn't be allowed. She should be ashamed of herself," and he would continue his rapt gaze.

If we apprentices had a complaint, we would go to Dougie; if he thought it legitimate, he would use his authority on our behalf. For example, on one occasion we had to vacate our cabin while it was being painted. The Chief Steward put us in a little-used cabin on the main deck that had poor ventilation, and was dirty and very hot. When we complained to Dougie, he told the Chief Steward to put us in one of the vacant passenger cabins on an upper deck. He was generous and sometimes in port he would give us apprentices money to do what we otherwise could not afford to do. On another occasion, by contrast, when he found some of us throwing around a heavy medicine ball for exercise, he took it and dumped it overboard. His view on physical games was that they wasted energy better used on ship's work. We became careful to limit our various physical activities to when he was not around.

As Senior Apprentice I had the privilege of having a small cabin to myself, and did not have to relieve the other apprentices for meals. A disadvantage was that 4 p.m. to 8 p.m. was the time when officers from the other watches gathered on the after deck to socialize, and I missed these gatherings. However, by now I had developed a variety of activities to keep myself occupied in my spare time. Beside classical music, reading was a great resource, and after going through all of my own books I would borrow from other people. As a treat on Sundays, I would read aloud to myself one of Shakespeare's plays, in order to fully appreciate his wonderful use of language. I also played chess when I could find an opponent.

When *Elysia* was crowded with passengers, they monopolized the deck games and it was difficult to find ways of getting exercise. Several of us enjoyed boxing. At first we were careful not to hit too hard, but as we gained skill we lost our reserve and went at it hammer and tongs. When the ship was rolling, we needed the additional skill of keeping our balance and using the roll to our advantage. Apart from some bloody noses and cut lips, we never inflicted much damage. Skipping was another good way of getting into training and letting off steam. Passengers would sometimes ask to join in, and this could lead to competitions with them. We were not allowed to dance with the passengers, but one evening, while down for supper, I had a dance with Miss Chambers, one of the stewardesses, whom I met in the saloon. The passengers were dancing up on deck, and by going into the galley we could hear the music plainly through the ventilator. We pushed a big cauldron of stock, fat and other mysterious slops into a corner, leaving just enough room to dance. We had some enjoyable waltzes and fox trots. Then a lump of fat stuck to Miss Chambers's shoe, almost causing a disaster when she skidded and nearly went head first into next day's soup. Then we got tangled among the works of the ice cream freezer, but these mishaps only added to the fun.

Several times we encountered rough weather that on previous voyages would have made me seasick. It was wonderful that I seemed to have got over the malady that on previous voyages had made me miserable.

While at Bombay I had, as usual, to spend many hours down the holds, seeing that the cargo was not broached. At times when there were breaks in the work I persuaded the Pathan stevedores to join with me in arm wrestling and obstacle races over hurdles made of bales of cotton. We had no common language, but I thought that they might enjoy the sound and rhythm of nursery rhymes. When I recited a few, the Pathans were delighted and asked me to teach them some. They learned quickly and repeated them as a group.

One of the holds contained metal drums, and when we started unloading we found they were leaking chlorine gas. I went down the hold and came up after less than five minutes with sore eyes, a running nose and a cough. The gas became so bad that six Pathan stevedores were blinded and many started spitting blood. Some of the stevedores had to be taken to hospital. It seemed incredible that the Pathans stuck it down the hold all morning, and the way they were driven by their foremen was inhuman and revolting. The work stopped only when the foremen concluded that the gas might injure the men so badly that it would mean a shortage of labour in the future for working other ships. During the afternoon "Burra Sahibs" (big shots) came aboard: the Anchor Line agents, representatives of the ICI and a naval expert on gas. They recommended rigging wind sails into the hold to try to vent some of the gas. Next day it was decided that some men from the Royal Indian Navy would unload the drums wearing general service gas masks. I greatly admired the English naval commander of these navy men. He was down with them, stripped to the waist, working as hard as anyone, and setting a fine example. Later, a gang of Pathans joined them, wearing masks we had improvised for them, and that we frequently cleaned with diluted Lysol and fresh water. The gas caused a delay of several days before all the drums were discharged.

One evening, a crane used in discharging cargo got tangled with the ship's wireless aerial. After trying all sorts of methods to clear it, I climbed up the arm of the crane, unshackled the aerial, tied a line onto the heavy porcelain conductors and lowered them down to the deck. It was a welcome change from routine cargo work to be able to do something adventurous.

Voyage 6 – January to March 1939

The sextant, used for measuring the angle between the horizon and the sun or stars, is an essential instrument for navigation that every officer in the deck department owns. It was now time that I should have a sextant, and while home on leave my father gave me money to buy one. While at Liverpool outward bound our new Captain kindly selected a second-hand sextant for me. Although it was made in 1903 it was very accurate. The Captain now expected me to hand in our daily noon position and my calculations, based on the sextant angle, time from the chronometer and nautical tables, gave a position that agreed closely with the Mate's. I was excited to know that now I could determine the ship's position.

I continued to be on the 4 to 8 watch with Dougie. Mr MacVicar had been transferred back to *Elysia* but I was no longer on watch with him. While passing through the Straits of Gibraltar, we watched a mock battle of British naval ships. Great battleships slid past us like shadows, then a battery of searchlights sprang into life, combing the darkness until they found their prey. Destroyers raced past, cutting close across our bows; overhead we heard the roar of planes and saw flares slowly dropping to earth. As it grew lighter we could make out warships of all sizes, each large one attended by two or three destroyers that fussed around like excited terriers. At a signal, they would leap forward belching smoke from their sterns and then swing around, hiding themselves in the veil of their own production. As the smoke cleared, three seaplanes approached the battleships, diving down over them and dropping flares instead of bombs. When finally the sun rose, the fleet slipped back into port as though afraid of the day.

Free time in port was limited by the demands of supervising the loading and unloading of cargo and other jobs given us by the mates. Normally we could expect only a few hours a day when we could go ashore. When free at Bombay, we went to Mission dances, explored the sights and markets, bought presents for family and friends, and swam at Breach Candy. For Scots, soccer was the major national game, and this being Scottish ship, many of us had played soccer since childhood. We had talked of playing so I bought a soccer ball, and during lunch breaks and early evenings a few of us would practise on a clear space on the dock using a warehouse door as a goal. Soon other crew members joined in. Later, when we were at Karachi, the Anchor Line agent told us that the *City of Benares*, a crack liner of the Ellerman City line, had challenged us to a match. As they had a much larger crew, no one on our ship except us apprentices much wanted to play. We gained the moral support of Mr MacVicar, our best player, and he persuaded the rest of the team to play.

Next evening we met with their team at the local soccer field. Our opponents all wore the same uniform and proper football boots. None of our team had football boots and we must have looked a scraggly lot, wearing a selection of old shorts, shirts or singlets and shoes. When they told us they had only lost two matches we began to feel that we were foolish to play them. During the first half we played with the wind, and at half time there was no score. During the second half we had a great fight, and to our delight Mr MacVicar scored a goal. After that we managed to keep our opponents from scoring until the final whistle blew. As we had expected them to walk over us, we were very excited at the result. We returned to the ship for a late tea. We were in the best of spirits, all sitting at the same table and for short time forgetting differences in rank. It was the most enjoyable meal I had had since joining *Elysia*.

During our stop at Aden, we were as usual besieged by merchants hawking their wares from the boats they brought alongside. By now I had gained experience in bargaining with them, and if I liked a passenger I would offer to buy on their behalf and secure a better price than they could get. It was an accepted practice that the merchants sold their goods at lower prices to members of the crew than they did to passengers, and I had become friendly with some of the merchants. I was still not supposed to converse with passengers, but as baggage master I met passengers and knew ways of evading the rule about not talking to them.

When we got back to England we learned that Germany had occupied Czechoslovakia. We were deeply concerned that this was yet another step towards the outbreak of the war we feared might come.

Voyage 7 – April to July 1939

Dougie's impairments of hearing and vision were becoming more apparent and he found it painful to stand for long periods. Our new Captain was very good to him, relieving him for the first hour of the afternoon watch by keeping watch for him, and no longer expecting him to hand in a noon position. His thoughtfulness seemed to make Dougie more confident, and Dougie became less critical of us apprentices. Earlier captains had often told Dougie off, making him afraid that he might be reported for inefficiency and possibly even be fired. Because of his older age, it might be difficult for him to get another job. While the Captain was relieving Dougie, he would sometimes talk with me and would tell me about his life at sea. He was always interesting, and time would pass more quickly.

Travelling eastward through the Straits of Gibraltar, we again watched naval manoeuvres but this time it was the German fleet. Two destroyers were carrying out a running fight, firing at each other with their gun sights set so that their salvos fell astern of each other. They were an impressive sight – probably the reason why the Germans held their manoeuvres in such a busy shipping lane. In anticipation of war all our officers were asked to study an admiralty publication, *The Defence of Merchant Shipping*.

On our passage from Gibraltar to Marseille we no longer had to stay away from the Spanish coast, since the Spanish civil war had ended on 1 April. Several times during this voyage we encountered rough weather that on previous voyages would have made me seasick. It was wonderful that I seemed to have got over the malady that on previous voyages had made me miserable.

Crossing the Arabian Sea, we again had to suffer the effects of the monsoon. There was little we could do except read and sleep in our spare time because of the wild movement of the ship, the heat and the humidity. As we came alongside the dock at Bombay, where the passengers were to disembark, the Pathan stevedores were waiting to take off the passengers' baggage. I was up on the forecastle with Dougie. When they saw me they waved and in chorus recited "Dickery dickery dock, the mouse ran up the clock", the nursery rhyme I had taught them on our previous stay at Bombay. I was amused to see the look of incredulity on the faces of the passengers.

At Bombay we were keen to play more soccer. After tea we would go ashore and practise until it grew too dark to see. It was terribly hot and we would return to the ship covered with dust and soaked with sweat. We challenged a German ship at soccer, and after some hesitation they accepted. For this trip we had bought, when at Glasgow, navy blue jerseys and white shorts. Our opponents had red jerseys decorated with the company's shield and the German eagle and swastika. Before the game began, they gave the Nazi salute. We won four goals to one, and at the end we gave three cheers and they gave three "Heils". Excited at the result, we invited their team to have supper with us. We were able to have some communication using our bad German and their bad English, and they stayed until nearly midnight.

The high temperature and humidity at Bombay were unrelenting. We complained to Dougie about the heat in our cabins, and he arranged for us to move to cooler ones in the passenger accommodation. One day Cowie, the apprentice, fainted from the heat while down in one of the holds. On the return trip to England from Bombay we carried troops and their families, either going home on leave or to a home station. One of the reasons that passengers liked *Elysia* was that she was a one-class ship, avoiding the invidious distinctions and snobbery found on ships segregated into classes based on income and social status. Unfortunately, to comply with the segregation of officers and men required by the army, we had to convert *Elysia* into a two-class ship. At meals, officers and their wives were at one sitting and the men and their wives at another. The two-class arrangement did not make for a happy ship.

Voyage 8 – September to November 1939

When Britain declared war on Germany on 3 September, we were steaming eastward in the Mediterranean. The navy had put on board sealed orders that were only to be opened at the outbreak of war. When the Captain opened them, he learned that we were to go to the nearest port where there was a British consul. We headed for Bizerte in Tunisia on the North Africa coast and lay offshore while the Second Mate went ashore in the ship's boat in search of the Consul. Several hours later he returned and reported that when he had found the Consul and explained his mission, the Consul replied, "My God, has the war started?" He knew nothing about instructions for us.

Our Captain then decided to steer for the island of Malta, a British naval base, in the hope that they would give us instructions. As we came to the mouth of the harbour a British naval launch came within hailing distance and told us to come no nearer and get back to sea. We obeyed, but were worried because we believed that Italy would declare war and become a German ally, and we were uncomfortably close to Italy. Fortunately they remained neutral and we reached Port Said, where we piled sandbags around the bridge for protection against attacks.

We continued on our usual round of visits to Bombay, coastal ports and Karachi to discharge and load cargo. On our homeward passage we joined a convoy from Gibraltar to Liverpool. The passage was stressful because we feared a submarine attack. One day we felt the ship shudder as though she had hit some heavy submerged object. This was our first experience of feeling the explosion of a depth charge. Soon after I intercepted a message Morsed from a destroyer to the convoy Commodore: "The enemy was only fish." Their ASTEC, an instrument they used for detecting underwater objects, had found a shoal of fish. When we reached Liverpool a 4.7-inch gun of ancient vintage was mounted on the stern of *Elysia* and I was one of the crew chosen to take a course of instruction in its use. The blackout made it difficult to find our way about when ashore. People were carrying gas masks and police were wearing steel helmets; there were more gun emplacements around the docks, and we now frequently saw men in uniform.

After discharging cargo at Liverpool and Manchester we proceeded to the Firth of Clyde, where we picked up a pilot who took us to an anchorage. We were to remain there overnight in order to take the flood tide next morning for our passage up the river to Glasgow. During the night a strong gale blew up with gusts of hurricane force. Since we had little cargo in our holds, having discharged most of it in Liverpool, much of our hull was above water and exposed to the wind. Our anchors started dragging and we were within shouting distance of the shore before the Captain, going ahead on the engine to reduce the strain on the anchors, was able to get *Elysia* clear of the shore. The anchorage was crowded with ships, many dragging their anchors, and we nearly hit a destroyer. Every time we dropped the anchors they started dragging, until shortly after 3 a.m. we ran aground on to a sandbank and *Elysia* listed heavily to starboard. It was several days before tugs were able to pull her free and we were able to proceed to Glasgow. Fortunately the grounding caused little damage.

Voyage 9 – December 1939 to March 1940

We took on passengers and cargo at Liverpool and were fortunate to make the passage to the Mediterranean without any sign of enemy action. To keep up with the timetable given in my correspondence course, I set myself a number of hours each week for studying. In extreme heat or very rough weather this was difficult to stick to and sometimes impossible, so when good weather returned I would try to make up for lost time. At the end of each voyage I sent what I had done to the College, and later got back their critique of my work. Because how much I studied was entirely up to me, I learned more about how to study than I had ever learned at school. I don't have a good memory and found it difficult to learn the lengthy international rules of the road.

It was on this voyage that I met Janet Mackay. I had first heard about her from the new Third Mate, Wee Jimmy. He told me that a Miss Mackay had been making inquiries about me. I thought nothing of it, but later he pointed her out to me walking round the deck with her mother. I was very struck by her appearance and told Wee Jimmy that she was one of the few girls I thought really good-looking.

Christmas Eve came, a lovely, calm night with a full moon and a warm breeze. The passengers were dancing out on deck. On our evening watch, Wee Jimmy and I were wild at not being able to join in the dancing. I told him that if I had been allowed to dance, Janet would have been my choice every time. Jimmy laughed at me, saying I would be lucky to get a single dance as she was very popular. I spent a miserable Christmas, feeling very homesick, because there was nothing out of the ordinary for us apprentices, not even having dinner with the passengers. Although I heard a fair amount about Janet from different sources, I hardly saw her in the western Mediterranean as she was in bed with the "*Elysia* throat", a sickness that was running riot through the ship. On New Year's Eve dancing started at midnight, and although I felt like joining in, that would have been most unwise without the Captain's permission. I was sorry that Janet was ill in bed as I would have risked his displeasure for a dance with her.

By the time we reached Port Said I still had not spoken to Janet, but I had plenty of opportunities to watch her and liked everything about her. She was tall, with black curly hair, a sweet face and a very charming manner. After Suez I began looking for opportunities to speak to her, but either could not think of anything to say when an opportunity arose or did not see her when I had thought of something to say. One morning I met her on the galley deck, teaching a baby to walk. Both of us must have been equally shy, as we only exchanged a few commonplace remarks. During the next few days I quite often spoke to Janet's mother, who was the first passenger to wish me a happy New Year. The Saturday before reaching Bombay I came from tea and saw Janet standing out on deck and stopped to speak to her, using as an opening remark that there had been an incorrect date on the report to the passengers of the distance the ship had travelled over the past 24 hours. We talked on and were still on deck when Janet's mother came to look for her.

The following evening we arranged to meet again, and we talked about our attitude towards the war. We seemed to stimulate each other's thought; I found it easy to express my ideas and to think quickly and with great clarity. I was a pacifist and Janet's father was in the Royal Navy. We were both willing and interested to hear the other's point of view. We also talked about other topics such as our families, our schools and our interests. After tea on the Monday evening of the farewell party I saw Janet for an hour or so, but she had to leave early in order to change. I asked her to meet me at 10 o'clock, when I came down for supper, so that I might see her in her evening dress. There was dancing during the evening and I so wanted to dance. I was not permitted to, and Janet said she didn't feel like dancing with anyone else. I came below at 10 o'clock and waited a few minutes in the saloon until Janet came in on the pretence of getting a glass of water. I left the saloon and she followed. By this time we had become very fond of each other and she told me she had been trying to get to know me all through the voyage.

Tuesday evening was our last opportunity to see each other. Time seemed to fly until the dinner gong went. Before Janet left, she suddenly kissed me and asked me whether I thought her an awful ass. I didn't, and said so, and she left me, crying.

During the first two hours of the watch the *Elysia* was approaching the entrance of the swept channel leading into Bombay; it was touch and go whether I would get down for supper at 10 p.m. My luck was in though, and at 10 o'clock all was quiet, so I met Janet at the same place. We did not speak much because we seemed to know each other's thoughts and it was sufficient happiness that we were together. She told me that she was terribly in love with me, and by the way she said it, I knew that it was true. I told her that I had always been looking for an ideal and that she had made that ideal come alive. That half hour was like a wonderful dream, and looking back on it I can hardly believe it really happened. Before I returned to the bridge we said goodbye, as we would hardly see each other the following morning, when she would leave the ship. For the first time I kissed a girl. I had known a great many other girls but never wanted to kiss any of them, but now it felt like a perfectly natural thing to do. Looking back, it seemed strange that after just a few hours together we had become so fond of each other. She was going with her mother to Calcutta to join her father. I wondered whether, if we met again, we would be disillusioned. At Bombay and the coastal ports I tried to keep busy and not think too much about her.

The time we spent on the Indian coast was when we worried least about the war. Everyone was in a good humour. I spent several mornings with the Captain strengthening the battlements on the bridge, and it was great fun working with him. He told me stories, true and untrue, pulled my leg, tried to catch me out with questions, and told me what work to do and how to do it. The work mainly consisted of carpentry, and as the Captain used to be a ship's carpenter, I learned a lot.

One evening at Karachi, the Third Engineer got a party of us to go on a sailing dhow he had hired. As soon as we were out in the harbour, the sail caught the breeze and we scudded along at a great rate. When the dhow heeled as the wind strengthened, a plank was pushed out and secured on the weather side, and the crew members sat out on the plank to counteract the heeling. I soon grew tired of sitting on the cushioned seats in the stern, and joined the men sitting out on the plank. Then I tried the experiment of making myself fast to one end of a rope, securing the other end to the boat and then jumping into the water. Being towed at seven or eight knots was an excellent substitute for a bath and quite exciting, because it was difficult to keep my face clear of the water. The best procedure was to lie on my back or side and look astern.

The daylight was fading, and gave way to a glorious tropical night of bright starlight and a new moon sinking slowly towards the horizon. We sailed across a stretch of water sheltered from the sea by a low spit of sand dunes and then landed. With Bhatchu (the Captain of the sailing dhow) as guide, we crossed the dunes to the seashore where great rollers were tumbling in over smooth firm sand. We raced along in the shallow water like high-stepping horses, kicking up great showers of spray and getting soaked in the process. The beach was swarming with white crabs, but as long as no light was shown they were not noticeable. Mrs Bagnol, a stewardess, was running ahead when I flashed on a torch. The circle of light illuminated crabs of all sizes and made Mrs Bagnol aware of them. She made a great and sustained effort to overcome gravity, giving a demonstration of acrobatic dancing which would have been the envy of a ballerina. The electrician gallantly came to her rescue with a pair of shoes.

We found marks in the sand as if a heavy tractor had come up out of the sea. We followed the tracks and found a great turtle that blinked in perplexity at the sudden glare of light from a torch. Probably it had come ashore to lay its eggs. We returned to the dhow pleasantly tired and settled down to enjoy the sail back. I lay looking up at the great dark sail and lazily identifying familiar stars. We enjoyed singing, and sang in chorus or solo until we it was time to leave the dhow and return to *Elysia*.

The homeward passage to England was uneventful. At that time, being unsure of censorship rules, I did not record anything about matters related to convoys and enemy action, but in the passage from Gibraltar to Liverpool, where this was most likely to have occurred, I have no memory of the convoy or whether it was attacked.

Voyage 10 – April to July 1940

With the growing threat of war, I had left my clarinets at home for safekeeping. I missed playing them and listening to music. So despite the risk of losing them through enemy action, I decided to bring my clarinets back to the ship with me. Cowie had been transferred to another ship so I no longer had the use of his piano accordion. I had a portable wind-up gramophone and a collection of records at home, and I brought those along as well.

Because of the additional work for the deck department owing to wartime conditions, our shipping company decided to add a Fourth Mate to our complement of deck officers and I was moved to the 8 to 12 watch. We also had a new Second Mate and Third Mate.

While in convoy in the Bay of Biscay, we were disturbed by depth charges exploding. Now that I knew the cause of the explosions they did not disturb me, but it must have been very upsetting for our passengers. When the Commodore of the convoy signalled an emergency, we mustered all the passengers on the promenade deck, wearing their life jackets. They had nothing to do but wait and fear what might happen. I could watch them from my vantage point on the gun platform at the stern. A woman passenger, known to be a heavy drinker and generally not making much sense, suddenly snapped out of her stupor and went round comforting women who were visibly upset. Nothing further happened and we stood down from the gun. I talked with crew members about German submarines. They did not show hatred of the men on them, but rather spoke of their admiration for their courage. The term I heard our crew apply to them most often was "big hearted".

When all was quiet on the bridge, I often relived memories of my time with Janet. As the voyage progressed, we apprentices found the new Second Mate was uninterested in our training, gave us stupid jobs, expected us to work longer hours off watch and was generally unpleasant to us. We avoided a bad row, but were always very close to the wind. I wish I could have found out why he disliked me so. It occurred to me that being an apprentice is, in some ways, rather like being a butler. I couldn't contradict orders, and it was advisable to remain pleasant and unruffled on all occasions, agreeing at least outwardly with what the Second Mate said. It was difficult armour for him to penetrate with sarcasm and criticism. Finally, we apprentices felt it was time to get our own back on the Second Mate. We knew that he was vain about his appearance and thought himself a ladies' man, so we developed a plan and persuaded some young women passengers to cooperate. One of them aroused the Second Mate's curiosity by looking at his hair. He asked why, and after some persuasion she told him that he had a distinctive hairline that indicated premature baldness. During the next few days, other women told him the same thing. To our delight, at the next port we found that the Second Mate had bought some hair restorer.

Sometimes I would drop in to the stewardesses' room for a chat. One day a small girl, Agnes, brought in her doll, which had had an accident and received severe head injuries. It was old, but Agnes was very fond of it, so I promised to try to repair the damage. Allwood, another apprentice, and I had an enjoyable hour sticking the pieces of head together with adhesive tape and glue. The result was fairly satisfactory, but there were scars, which were rather noticeable. We forced putty into the scars, and after it dried tried to colour it like skin. Agnes was very happy with our operation.

Some wireless news came through for the first time since we had left England. Germany had attacked Denmark and Norway, but we were not told whether there was resistance. There was also news of British naval and air force raids on German ships at Narvick and other Norwegian harbours. When we reached Aden there were many Danish and Norwegian ships, presumably awaiting orders as they had been taken over by the British Admiralty. I heard, from a not too reliable source, that the Germans were putting pressure on the crews of these ships not to cooperate with the British by threatening to confiscate their property and victimize their families.

When we reached Bombay we heard rumours that we might have to sail round Africa. We made our usual visits to ports on the Indian coast and sailed from Karachi with a full load of cargo and a few passengers. Arriving at Aden on 19 May, we were told to await orders.

There was a continuous flow of launches carrying women and children out to two passenger ships, which were to evacuate them to Bombay. The jetty ashore was packed with people and baggage waiting to get away. Later we learned that a reason for the precipitous evacuation was that Italian planes had flown over Aden. Near us a British battleship was going through her Sunday routine. I could see the band parading on the after deck, and an inspection that was accompanied by much marching to and fro. They then had a church service.

After a few days we received orders to go round Africa. We expected our passage to Cape Town to take about 18 days. Our fresh water tanks were too small for such a long passage. As a result, water had to be rationed. Our first few days at sea were unpleasant, with a heavy south-west swell and high humidity and temperatures. We were relieved when the weather changed to a gentle breeze with calm seas. About this time we received a wireless message reporting that there were several German raiders at large in our vicinity disguised as Japanese ships. During the Second Mate's watch, he sighted a Japanese ship and called the Captain, who altered course away from her. She continued on her course, and when she made no attempt to follow us we became satisfied she was not a raider.

We were to make our first crossing of the equator on 25 May, and preparations were made for the traditional ceremony. However, one of the passengers told the Old Man that she would sue the company if she were ducked, so he cancelled the ceremony. I hated to think that crossing the equator should go unnoticed and decided to do something about it. I told my fellow apprentice Marshall to come down from the bridge at one o'clock, when Allwood and I planned to duck him with the help of Kennedy, a quartermaster. Unfortunately the swimming pool was empty, so I rigged a hose on the after deck. Allwood was in uniform when he came off watch. We allowed him time to change into old clothes, then frogmarched him out on deck and thoroughly soused him with the salt water from the hose. During the operation we all got soaked. Once started, everyone who had been soaked was eager to find new victims. We found the stewardesses and carried them to the place of execution. Before we had finished, quite a number of the passengers had been dealt with. Douglas, the Butler, ran to take refuge in the dining saloon, only to have several dripping figures wearing just a pair of shorts in full pursuit. We captured him and dragged him off, to the great amusement of the passengers who were having lunch. We carefully avoided the passenger who had threatened to sue the company.

To make the time pass faster, the Captain organized a games tournament of deck golf, deck tennis and shuffleboard. Each passenger was given a crew member as a partner. I was picked to play with a Mr Simpson who looked as though he might be good. The only drawback to my participation was Dougie, the Chief Officer, who disliked my taking any form of exercise except work. I did not like to go against his wishes, but because the Captain organized the tournament Dougie was in no position to prevent my playing. In a doubles deck tennis match against very good players, my partner and I were able to win only because one of our opponents had had a good deal to drink and seemed to be attempting to catch the wrong one of the two quoits he was apparently seeing. I had an advantage over the passengers when the ship was rolling, because I had sea legs and could keep my balance better than they.

Living within the confines of the ship, we only received fragments of wireless news about the war and what we did hear was bad. On 28 May we learned that the Germans were advancing fast in France, having occupied Boulogne, and were nearing Calais. On the 31st we heard that the Germans had captured Calais after a brave defence by a small number of British troops. Italy was going ahead with preparations for war, and on 4 June the news came that the Germans were bombing Paris and Marseille.

The Second Mate continued to be a source of annoyance. For example, he told me to chip rusty paint in the wheelhouse. I was in white tropical uniform, so went down and changed into working clothes. When I returned, he ordered me to change back into uniform. I objected, saying that no laundry was allowed owing to the shortage of water and I was short of spare uniforms Nevertheless, he made me change back so I changed into the dirtiest uniform I had. On another occasion I was doing some painting for him when off watch and put in the hour's work he had set for me. When I went to my cabin to study he called me back to the bridge and made me finish the painting. He took not the slightest interest in our learning to become officers, and felt that our work for the ship had nothing to do with our training. Finally, I asked to speak to him about his statement that there were no restrictions on our working hours, and no grounds on which to complain if we worked long hours. I then read him this extract from our indentures: "The first parties (i.e. Anchor Line Ltd.) hereby bind and oblige themselves to use all proper means to cause the said Midshipman to be taught the business of Seaman and the duties of a Navigating Officer." I told him he was not fulfilling this obligation and was giving us no instruction. The Second Mate replied: "Are you trying to tell me what work I have to give you?" I replied, "Yes." At this he lost his temper and shouted that he would not listen to another word. I then told him that if he refused to discuss what work we should do, I would bring the matter up with the Captain and, if necessary, with the Anchor Line main office. This encounter had some effect, as he became less obnoxious and more reasonable in the amount and kind of work he gave us.

As we steamed south, the weather became cooler and we changed into our heavier blue uniforms. For the first time I saw albatrosses. They glided in great sweeps and curves, their only movement being a slight alteration to the curve of their wings. They had wingspans of about eight feet; their bodies were white underneath and their wings a mixture of grey, white and black. Their seemingly effortless flight was beautiful to watch, and sometimes they hovered only a few feet above our heads. The birds when on land take off from a crag or pinnacle, and when on the water they slowly gather speed by paddling and then take off from the crest of a wave.

When we reached the latitude of the south coast of Africa, we had to keep outside the one thousand fathom line and steam several hundreds of extra miles to the south in order to avoid the mines the Germans had laid on the Agulhas Bank near to the coast. The temperature dropped to near freezing point, with a heavy southerly long swell, and several times we shipped seas that on one occasion soaked passengers who were playing deck golf on the fore deck.

We reached Cape Town on 6 June, remaining in port only long enough take on oil, water and supplies. We were on our way again the following day, heading for Freeport, Sierra Leone. This passage was largely uneventful. The first few days were cold with some swell, but as we entered the tropics we changed back again into white tropical uniforms and *Elysia* stayed on an even keel. It was good weather for deck games, sunbathing and listening to gramophone records out on deck. Off watch we apprentices had the pleasant task of checking the gear in the lifeboats, where we could sunbathe and go at our own pace. As usual I read a great deal, and played my clarinets. I tried to keep to my self-imposed schedule of studying for the exams that I would take when my apprenticeship finished.

We continued to receive bad news about the war. On 10 June a message came in from the Admiralty: "War will commence with Italy at 0001. British Summer Time. Tuesday 11. June." The wording somehow seemed out of place and sounded more like an announcement of a football match. I didn't know whether it was perhaps the Captain's response to this news, but he found three passengers who knew about guns and brought them up on the bridge to try out our antiquated rifles, perhaps in the somewhat vain hope that they might repel the enemy. He also ordered us to fire practice shots with our aged 4.7-inch gun, which was mounted at the stern. A target was thrown overboard, and by the third shot our aim had improved and we got near it.

On 15 June we learned that the German army had entered Paris. On the 18th the Wireless Operator reported that France had laid down her arms and asked for an armistice and that Britain would fight on. He had just finished receiving the news when he was disturbed by a call to action stations. We had sighted what at first looked like a shoal of fish, but using a telescope we could see a wake moving through the water; there was a track of broken water and bubbles, and something projecting from the water that looked unlike a large fish and suspiciously like the periscope of a submarine, The Old Man swung the ship's head away from the broken water and rang for top speed. I collected the gun crew and within a minute or two we had the gun ready for action. All hands were mustered on deck and the passengers were ordered to put on their lifejackets. We slowly pulled away from the object in the water and after an hour we were given the order to stand down. The incident stimulated conversation to a remarkable degree.

Occasionally an informal party would start in someone's cabin. One day I went into the stewardesses' cabin to see if I could borrow some black wool to darn my socks. Miss Graham, a passenger who had been matron at a Calcutta Hospital, was in the cabin and, since I was followed by Marshall and the Fourth Engineer and Fifth Engineer, she asked us all to have a drink. After some chitchat, Miss Graham started us singing and kept the party going. She was middle-aged, small and rather fierce looking, with a heavily lined face and large, powerful hands. She took a great delight in swearing, and when she was at work she must have been an imposing, terrifying character. As it was, she appeared very fond of nagging, quite often having a friendly scrap with Mrs Bagnol, one of the stewardesses, who invariably got the worst of it. Miss Graham kindly offered to darn my socks.

After a 13-day passage from Cape Town, we picked up a Freetown pilot and entered the broad mouth of the Sierra Leone River. The estuary was crowded with shipping waiting for a convoy to form. After picking our way through the ships, we anchored and remained for eight days waiting for the convoy to sail. While at anchor we learned that there had been the first big air raid on Britain with 12 people killed and 36 injured. We feared that worse was to come.

While at anchor at Freetown, I was intrigued by the dugout canoes that came alongside. The men in the canoes were dressed in ragged old shirts and singlets and had to paddle hard to breast the strong current. Their narrow canoes were beautifully shaped and were filled with goods for sale, such as baskets, fruit, live chickens, a few monkeys, and some cheap torches and coloured handkerchiefs. Our sailors seemed more eager to exchange their wares for old clothes than money and, amidst a confused din of bargaining most of the old clothes on our ship passed into the Africans' hands. Among the wares bought were three scraggly looking chickens that strutted round the decks to the excitement of the two dogs on board.

I was intrigued with the idea of buying a canoe and taking it home, having learned that I could get one for less than £2 ($8.00). I asked and received the Old Man's and the Chief Officer's permission to carry one home on the ship. After lunch I was given leave to go ashore, and I enquired where the canoes were built. An Englishman put me on the track and a local boy volunteered to act as my guide. I passed a crowd of African girls, presumably all from the same school because they all wore blue frocks. Some of the women wore European frocks, but most of them only wore a piece of coloured cloth as a skirt. A woman went by carrying a baby on her back, baskets in both hands and another large one on her head! My guide led me to a narrow river, beside which lay a group of wattle huts. The only indications of European influence in the village were a few Trilby hats worn by the men, some English-style shirts and a cricket blazer, all of which seemed incongruous in the overall African setting of the village.

I met the headman of the village, and after some preliminary talk asked him if I could buy a canoe. They were mostly located across the river, so he insisted on carrying me across on his back. Although small in stature he was immensely strong, with broad shoulders, a short, thick neck and a deep chest. He laughed a lot. I had difficulty in finding the canoe I wanted: some were new but had flaws in the wood or were cracked, some were so narrow that I could not get my hips into them, and some were too heavy. Eventually I found one that I liked, and after much talk we agreed that the headman would deliver it alongside *Elysia* and I would pay him 30 shillings ($6) and a jersey. By the time that I got back to *Elysia*, the headman and canoe were waiting for me. We hoisted the canoe aboard, and as the headman had brought the canoe to the ship, I added a tie to the deal and put it on for him. He was really pleased, and indeed we were both delighted with the whole transaction.

We were able to get oil fuel for the ship, but it was difficult to get all the water we needed, as there was a local shortage. Accordingly, the Chief Officer ordered the awnings rigged to catch rainwater. The following days there were torrential downpours, and we collected several hundred gallons of water, filling buckets from the edge of the awnings. We also used the opportunity to bathe in the rain.

My twentieth birthday was on 24 June but it went unnoticed by others. I celebrated by listening to my favourite records. The Old Man and Dougie went ashore for the convoy conference and we had a busy morning getting things ready because we had been chosen as commodore ship. The Commodore had overall command and responsibility for the conduct of the convoy, and he and his staff came aboard in the afternoon. Next morning we sailed, and when clear of the harbour the ships formed up as a convoy.

The stewardesses' cabin was something of a social centre for the officers. On one of my visits I found several people already there. The conversation turned as usual to the recent international news. Romania had ceded land to Russia, which was advancing with a great display of military force; Germany had occupied the Channel Islands, and merchant ships were being sunk in increasing numbers by submarines and enemy raiders. Everyone was gloomy, and we expected a rough time of it before we got home.

Dougie had been very depressed recently; he thought that Britain was being punished for her ungodliness, and that we would be beaten and have to suffer German domination. The stewardesses talked of "fighting to the last man" and preferring to be "shot rather than suffer the indignity of being ruled by a foreigner". I found it hard to know what to think, and preferred to remain silent at these discussions and listen to other people talk. I was clear only in my hatred of all war for whatever purpose, and in my determination to try to keep a sane outlook, and not to get carried away by narrow patriotism and propaganda. I felt sorrow for the stupid and senseless loss of life and the immense suffering on both sides.

A heavy swell arose and several big seas lapped over the bulwarks onto the after deck. I happened to be at the mouth of the alleyway when the first sea broke over. The hens, who were occupied as usual in picking at the rice which was left out for them, were taken by surprise, and stimulated by the shock of the water pouring over them rose into the air and flapped to the nearest point of safety. One hen flew up over the bulwarks, before making the unpleasant discovery that an endless vista of water stretched away from the ship. Acting with admirable presence of mind under the strain of the moment, she proceeded to perform some acrobatics that seemed a clumsy imitation of looping the loop, a half-roll and finally a clumsy pancake landing on top of a bulwark. Here she struggled desperately to maintain her balance, violently flapping her wings and using a stream of invective, the meaning of which I was fortunately ignorant of. Several of the nearby sailors watched, with deep concern, the near loss of next week's dinner.

Several of our crew were down with malaria. Other ships had the same problem. One ship in the convoy signalled over to the Commodore that so many of their crew had severe malaria that there were not enough hands to man the ship. The Commodore arranged for men from other ships to be transferred to help so that the ship could remain in the convoy.

During our stay at Freetown I was unable to get rid of a restless feeling that made me dissatisfied and unable to settle down to anything, but after returning to sea I enjoyed life more than usual, having plenty to do and getting it done. In my spare time I sanded and oiled the hull of the canoe and fitted new gunwales with the help of the ship's Carpenter.

The convoy was approaching the danger zone, and time on watch passed slowly. Continually watching the sea for signs of submarines became very wearisome. On the bridge, everyone was on edge. Extra lookouts had been posted. Our naval escort was several hours late in arriving and the Commodore was very worried. It must have been a tremendous strain on him, with his responsibility for managing the convoy and the long hours he spent on the bridge.

One evening an escort hoisted the danger signal. The Commodore altered the course of the convoy in order to bring the submarine astern and leave a clear space for the escorts to go hunting. We manned our gun and got soaked by pouring rain. During the long wait that ensued, there was the occasional dull explosion of a depth charge. Later the escorts rejoined us, signalling that they thought they had sunk the submarine because patches of oil had appeared.

As we were approaching England, a flying boat that was escorting us dropped four bombs, for reasons unknown to us. Again the danger signal went up on an escort, and again we went to action stations. The escort was sniffing around very close to us and the flying boat was circling overhead, but no bombs or depth charges were dropped. We surmised that shortage of depth charges and bombs was the reason. Everyone available was on the lookout for planes, submarines and enemy surface craft. Off Lands End, an air raid warning message was received. Later in the morning we passed a great smear of oil where a tanker had recently been torpedoed.

After having been on board *Elysia* for two months with only a few hours ashore, everyone was very restless (a state we usually called "the channels"). Passengers excitedly pointed out any signs of the English coast. The Pilot came aboard as we approached Liverpool, and soon after, came a host of officials. Far more important to us was the mail brought aboard. I was very relieved to learn that my parents were well and our home was intact and, to my delight, there was also a letter from Janet. The passengers were taken ashore in a tender, but because the docks were full we were ordered to go directly up the ship canal to Manchester to discharge our cargo. Our pilot for the canal appeared plain and insignificant, but he soon had everyone on the bridge in fits of laughter with stories about his life. We tied up overnight, and on the journey up the canal his stories and entertainment powers lasted until we reached Manchester on the afternoon of 14 July. From then until teatime I was jumping about like a cat on hot bricks, waiting to find out whether I was to get leave. Finally our shore passes came through, and Dougie said that I could go home.

On leave – July to August 1940

My original diary contains many pages devoted to the times I spent on leave from *Elysia*. Writing about those times gave me an opportunity to relive events on shore that I so missed at sea. Because this book is primarily about my experiences at sea, this is the only leave during my apprenticeship that I will describe.

For my first few days at home I did little of note, but found great enjoyment in going down town with Mother, helping Daddy paste muslin on the windows to prevent the glass from splintering during air raids, and spending time with my 13-year-old sister Elaine. During air raids she was plucky and cheerful, bringing in our dog Nansen from his kennel and then settling down in the hall while I read to her or played the gramophone.

One evening Daddy called a meeting at our house for everyone who lived on our street, in order to comply with a government order that each street plan to participate in air raid precautions. It was the first time everyone in our street had been together and the noise of conversation was so great that Daddy could not start the meeting. Suddenly there was a crash and everyone stopped talking to see what had happened. Daddy had deliberately fallen flat on the floor and used the silence to say, "That, ladies and gentlemen, is the correct procedure if you hear a bomb dropping. We will now start the meeting." Then he got up.

Our family had a small rented cottage that stood at the head of a meadow overlooking Loch Long. To reach the cottage we had to travel by train, a steamer across the Firth of Clyde and a local bus, and then walk several miles over sheep tracks or row in a small boat we kept at the village. I spent a few days at the cottage with my parents, Elaine, my brother Olaf and several friends. The facilities at the cottage were very primitive. On arrival we lit the stove, drew water from the burn (small stream), swept the rooms, collected firewood and cooked a meal. One of the treats at the cottage was long hours of sleep. It was a tradition for Mother and the girls to get up, light the stove and make early morning tea, while the males lay lazily gathering their senses together until tea was brought to them. Then we were allowed no peace until we got up and cooked breakfast.

The day after we arrived I went to meet a guest due to arrive by steamer at the nearest village. It was a grand day for walking, and since I had plenty of time I walked the whole way rather than taking the bus. It was the first good walk I had had in ages, and being able to walk fast and get into a swinging stride was a great joy. While waiting at the pier for the steamer I saw, in the direction from which the steamer would normally come, a great column of water shoot up several hundred feet in the air. I had been told that the previous night German planes had come over laying mines in the Firth and jumped to the conclusion that the column of water was caused by the steamer hitting a mine. My worry ended when the steamer hove in sight with our guest safely on board.

One morning some of us set off to climb the mountain behind the cottage. We followed up a track beside the burn and then plunged into thick undergrowth that stood shoulder high. By the time that we had climbed above the tree line to the rocky outcrops, we were ready to throw ourselves down in the heather and regain our breath. The lochs and mountains were looking their best, their colours changing as the white cumulus clouds moved across the sky. Nansen had little time for the view, either rolling among the heather with snores of contentment or lying close by, watching us with his muzzle between his paws. Several times we thought that we had reached the top, only to be disappointed as another shoulder rose above the skyline to taunt us. Eventually we reached the cairn of stones that marked the summit and followed the ritual of adding stones to it.

There was mixed opinion about swimming in the loch. We all swam, the greater enthusiasm being shown by the girls and Mother, and the greatest reluctance coming from my brother and me. Mother tried to encourage us by saying that swimming in cold water was good for the character.

One of our guests was Molly Gray. We had both been adopted and Molly liked to think that we might be sister and brother. We had known each other since we were children and were very fond of each other. While on a walk together, a remark of Molly's caused me a lot of thought. She said that I expected too much of people, and that if I accepted people for what they were, I would make more friends and get on more easily. She felt I should not give such exaggerated importance to literature and classical music, and should be able to delight in simple things.

When we returned to our home in Paisley I was recalled to the *Elysia*, berthed in Glasgow. It was some time before we sailed and I was given a half-day off so I could return home. I was eager to try out the dugout canoe I had brought home from Freetown. I had built a wheeled cart to carry it, so with Elaine used the half-day leave for the canoe's maiden voyage. We set off for a nearby river with me pulling the cart and Elaine holding a rope and acting as a brake. We reached the river, and I launched the canoe. But the canoe had other ideas, and after a few seconds rolled over, precipitating me into the slimy river. Each time I ventured back in, the canoe I would go a little further before upsetting. Elaine wanted a try, and her first voyage met with more success than mine. We played about until we got cold, then we dressed and returned home highly pleased with the expedition. So ended a delightful leave.

Voyage 11 – August 1940 to January 1941

After our passage from Glasgow to Liverpool, the loading of cargo went on day and night. Air raid warnings sounded almost every night, causing stoppages in the loading. On Friday I had been working until midnight. and had undressed and was just getting into bed when a whistling sound grew in a rapid crescendo, to be followed by a loud explosion. I grabbed a jacket and went out into the alleyway to put one more bulkhead between myself and the explosion from the next bomb that I expected to fall. Out on deck, the stevedores were climbing up out of the holds, the floodlights on the ship were extinguished and everyone made a run for cover as we heard the roar of German planes passing low overhead. The Fourth Mate wanted the Chief Officer called, so I went up on the bridge to warn him. I found he had come down inside the accommodation on the galley deck to get some protection, so I stayed with him.

The bomb we heard must have been aimed at the ship, illuminated by the working lights, but it had either fallen in the dock or had blown up some nearby houses. In the pitch darkness the men were all talking in a loud, excited manner. It was over a quarter of an hour after the first bomb dropped that we heard the wail of the air raid warning sirens. In the meantime, many more bombs had dropped fairly close by and the search-lights had been vainly trying to pierce the thick clouds behind which the planes were hiding. Once they caught a plane in their beams, a burst of anti-aircraft fire followed until the bomber dived back into the clouds. The reflection of the searchlights off the clouds lit up Liverpool. Eventually the all-clear siren sounded.

Our destination was Bombay, and again we were routed to go round Africa. On September 13 more than a hundred passengers, almost a full complement, embarked. At one o'clock the tugs pulled us clear of the berth and we moved to an anchorage. As soon as I was free I lay down and slept until teatime, making up for some of the sleep I had lost through night work and air raids. Later we left the anchorage and steamed down the river towards the Bar Light vessel. The convoy was gathering as we dropped anchor again. The pilot boats were busy running between the ships, taking off the pilots. Various signals told us that an air raid was expected ashore. Hundreds of searchlights sprang into life, their beams weaving in and out in intricate patterns as they searched the sky for enemy raiders. Then for a few minutes the sky to the east was dotted with balls of fire that quickly lost their shape and disappeared again. It was a beautiful sight in the distance, when we could see and hear nothing of the ter-ror and perhaps tragedy that lay below the spectacle.

Next morning under a grey sky, cut off from sight of land by a light drizzle, the con-voy formed up and started out along the channel which had been swept clear of mines. We knew our position in the convoy by a two-digit number given each ship before sail-ing. The first digit indicated the column numbered from left to right in which we were to sail, and the second digit was our position in the column numbered from front to back. We had a new Captain this voyage, Frank Henderson, a tall, well-built man with a quiet, confident, commanding air.

On the following evening at 8.30, Kennedy, a quartermaster, phoned the bridge to report that he had seen a periscope close on the starboard quarter. I took the report to the Old Man and found with him a passenger who had also seen the object in the water. There followed several minutes of frantic signalling, and I am ashamed to say that for a short time I was not concentrating on the Morse message I was sending. I was letting my-self get too excited. It wasn't until I had sent a wrong letter that I settled down to do the job properly. A little later, a depth charge was dropped close to us and we went to action stations. Nothing happened. During the long standby that followed I had nothing to do, so went into the gunners' room and read part of an adventure story about a secret German submarine base in the north of Scotland. (Most suitable literature for the occasion.)

Shortly before 10, we were told to stand down. When I returned to the bridge I learned that the Old Man had decided to set double watches (four hours on, four hours off). The Second Mate, Third Mate and myself were to take one watch, the Chief Officer, Fourth Mate and Marshall, an apprentice, the other. The third apprentice, Allwood, was to be on the bridge during daylight to help with the signalling. After going off watch at midnight, I was called at one bell to go on watch at 4 a.m., and spent the next four hours peering out into the darkness and later searching the water with binoculars as the daylight slowly changed the darkness into the dull grey of a misty, drizzly morning. One by one the ships in the convoy loomed into sight like silent spectres, indefinite in shape and detail, and then little by little assumed solid form. How aptly Masefield describes such a morning: "A grey mist on the sea's face and a grey dawn breaking." It was at dawn and dusk that submarine attacks were most likely, and a sharp watch had to be kept. Until we got back to our normal watches, we would be able to do little else but keep watch, eat and sleep. Not counting the Old Man, there were always 10 men on the lookout. On this voyage a route round the north of Ireland was made necessary because the Admiralty had laid mine fields right across the southern end of the Irish Sea to keep out German submarines. Our route also increased the distance that enemy planes would have to fly in order to attack us.

On 16 August the morning watch was passing quietly, and at 10 a.m. I went down to open the hatch for baggage day. We had nearly finished when there was a dull explosion. I happened to be looking out at the ships on the starboard beam and saw a column of water and black smoke rise from the far side of one of the ships. The Old Man was standing on the promenade deck talking to a passenger, and I drew his attention to the spot. As he was sheltered from the sound by the wind, he had not heard anything. By this time, the ship between us and the column of smoke no longer obstructed the view and we saw a small vessel in the centre of the convoy with a bad list to port that was rapidly getting worse. She had been torpedoed, and as the submerged submarine was in all probability taking aim at another vessel in the convoy, I gave the Bosun orders to cover the hatch and returned to the bridge as quickly as possible. The small cargo ship was sinking fast. Her stern sank out of sight and only her bows were above water. When I looked again, she had gone, sunk in a few minutes, without enough time for her crew even to get the lifeboats lowered.

It was a rotten sight, but I was too busy to think about it, running round the ship giving a succession of three long blasts on a whistle to muster the passengers at emergency stations, and muster the gun's crew. I woke up the Fourth Mate, who started to his feet with a concerned and startled expression as I dashed out again. After opening up the ammunition magazine and seeing the supply party ready to commence passing up shells and cordite to the gun, I returned to the bridge, and after reporting everything in order gave Allwood a hand with the signalling. At this emergency I made no mistakes, but was still annoyed at myself for becoming too excited earlier, when I tried to do things too quickly. I had forgotten the motto "More haste, less speed". My only excuse was that with such long hours on watch and broken sleep I might not have had as good a grip on myself as I generally do. Nothing further happened, and after a long period of waiting the Commodore sent up the flag hoist "Dismiss gun crews". Our naval escort had left, and because we were out on the port wing of the convoy, we were in one of the most vulnerable positions if attacked.

Shortly afterwards there was a loud explosion which shook the ship, and I raced across the bridge to see a large "Blue Funnel Line" cargo ship slew round with smoke rising from her fore deck and her bows low in the water. Her station was next to ours, and because she was very close to us, and the torpedo had struck her port side, the torpedo must have just missed us. Again, everyone was called to stations, although this time most of the passengers and crew had already rushed up on deck. A shot fired by the Vice Commodore's ship whistled across our bows. They must have sighted the U-boat, or estimated her approximate position, for the shell sent up a spout of water as it landed out on our port beam. We saw nothing of the submarine or the torpedo. For several minutes I was too busy preparing our gun and signalling to have a look round. When the first lull in activity occurred, I trained a telescope on the torpedoed ship which had dropped astern. She did not seem to have sunk much lower in the water and one of her lifeboats was standing by. The others were still hooked onto the davit falls and were hanging close to the water. Again, much to the surprise of most people, no second explosion occurred and the convoy steamed on at maximum speed with the ship detailed for rescue work remaining astern. Why the submarine did not take more advantage of such a golden opportunity, I don't know. We had no escort, and apart from our guns and smoke floats were entirely unprotected. The U-boat can't have known this and probably retreated as fast as possible for fear of depth charges.

Shortly before 2 p.m., the Commodore gave the order to stand down and everyone was able to get a late lunch. I ate with the passengers, many of them having undergone a remarkable recovery from seasickness! A tall girl sitting next to me kept up a running fire of questions such as "Why wasn't the Navy here?", "Why had we been put on the outside of the convoy, because surely it was wrong to put a passenger ship in one of the most dangerous positions?" and many others. They were excellent questions, to which I could not give satisfactory replies, and to which I think even the Admiralty could not have found valid answers. In addition, I was feeling very tired, with the one idea of turning in as quickly as possible. I replied rather curtly, and I hope I wasn't rude. For some reason, passengers thought our knowledge of submarine warfare was unlimited and swallowed without question anything they were told, spreading the information to everyone they met. It certainly made me think before replying.

When I came on watch again at four, the convoy had just been ordered to disperse and ships were proceeding in many different directions at their maximum speed. The low visibility, caused by a heavy grey sky and mist, was in our favour, and in a few hours no ships were to be seen. Several wireless messages came in during the next hour or so. A Clan Company ship from the convoy had been torpedoed a few miles to the south-east of us and two ships had sighted submarines. During the 8 to 12 watch the wind rose to almost gale force. The ship was pitching and straining and shipping heavy spray. By midnight I was blessing the inventor of tea, feeling that no price would be too high to pay for a hot bath, and a 12-hour sleep in a comfortable bed in a room with a coal fire burning. Instead, I had less than a four-hour sleep before turning out again after yesterday's 17-hour day on the bridge.

During the 4 to 8 a.m. watch next morning, a ship showed up on the horizon to the east travelling fast towards us. We were concerned that she might be a German raider, but as she approached we identified her as a British ship. There was a fine drizzle that made it difficult to keep a lookout without being blinded by rain, but it did help to hide us. At 4 p.m. we were put back on our usual watches.

For the remainder of our passage to Cape Town, only a few notable incidents disturbed our usual daily activities of work and leisure time. Because of the number of passengers, we had to call in at the Cape Verde Islands to replenish the water supply. These islands are in mid Atlantic, west of Senegal, West Africa. Shortly after leaving the islands the Carpenter sounded No. 1 bilge and found over four feet of water on the starboard side and nearly as much to port. The engine room pumps were immediately started and the sailors manned the hand pump, which was rigged on deck. There was no way of finding out what had caused the leak. It was not until the afternoon that any headway was made against the water, and evening came before the pumps gained on the inflow. From then on a close watch was kept to see that the leak did not get worse.

The Captain required us apprentices to take morning sights and hand in the ship's position each day. He kept an eye on our training, and we were no longer given tedious and meaningless jobs. Since he disapproved of our mixing with the passengers, we no longer played deck games with them. There were indications that the passengers were going to be more enterprising than on previous voyages. Committees were formed for sports and entertainment, and plans were afoot for games tournaments, weekly concerts, children's sports and treasure hunts. It often occurred at the beginning of a voyage that all sorts of plans were made for entertainment and then few were put into practice.

As we approached the equator the Captain gave the order to rig the salt-water hose on the fore deck. Knowing full well that these arrangements foretold the ritual of "crossing the line", I asked the Old Man whether we apprentices could assist with the ceremony and he gave his consent. At 10 a.m. a party made up of the apprentices and junior engineers went up onto the promenade deck, where the Second Mate pointed out to us our first victim. He was sitting in the smoke room, a tall, heavily built man. It took four of us to carry him down to the fore deck where he was soaked, to the vast amusement of the passengers who lined the forward end of the promenade deck. Their turn was to come though, and one by one they were singled out and dragged, carried, or escorted to the execution square. I became self-appointed executioner for the Captain, and consequently had the task of capturing most of the girls and carrying them to the hose. Some fought like cats, and during one scrap I had my singlet half torn off. I had never had the opportunity to go up to a girl whom I did not know, tell her curtly to take off her watch, and then pick her up and carry her, submissive or struggling, to a powerful hose where she was soused, clothes and all. My admiration rose for the villainous knights who carried off damsels, as I found transporting a pugnacious female was no mean undertaking. One Amazon required four men to subdue her and even then she put up a great fight. Some of the passengers locked themselves into the bathroom, but the Captain hit on the bright idea of using the stirrup pump, intended for extinguishing incendiary bombs, to pour water on them from over the top of the door. By the time 80 or 90 people had been dealt with, I was only too glad to stop work. Two days later the girl who had torn my singlet handed me an envelope containing a miniature singlet and a note: "So sorry a new one cannot be bought on board. This is the best substitute I can provide."

On 8 September the wireless news described an air raid on London in which 500 German planes took part. The attack started in daylight and was carried on continuously until early the following morning. The damage and the loss of life were appalling – 400 killed and 1400 injured! This was the first raid on such a large scale since the war began. It would be ghastly if they became a daily occurrence.

After a 32-day passage from Liverpool, we docked at Cape Town on 13 September for an overnight stay. We were on our way the next day, having taken on fuel and stores. By now the passengers had developed a variety of activities. They held weekly concerts, dances and deck games tournaments, and for the children organized a sports day, a fancy dress party and dancing lessons. For one of the concerts, the girls formed a chorus line and practised on the forecastle. We enjoyed watching some of these activities from the bridge. Some of the younger passengers organized a secret society, whose object was to liven up the ship by playing practical jokes. One of their jokes was to sew up the legs of the Captain's pyjamas. Some members attacked a boy, put a sack over his head and dumped him into a cold bath. I did not find out for what crime he was punished, but it was not my idea of a joke.

As we were nearing Bombay the Captain threw open the bridge for passengers, who came crowding up to be shown around. When some girls asked me to be their guide, I took them up on the monkey island (above the wheelhouse) because the wheelhouse and chartroom were full of people. After showing them how the azimuth mirror worked and explaining its uses, I stayed to show other people the compass. When I came down the girls were again without a guide, so I showed them round, teaching them some of the rudiments of signalling and how to handle a sextant. It made my morning watch pass quickly.

After being on board for two months, everyone welcomed our arrival at Bombay on 4 October. The passengers disembarked with their baggage and then we moved into the docks to the berth to unload cargo. When the mail was brought on board, I got a letter from Janet containing the great news that she was now in Karachi, where I would be able to see her.

Because of the leak, it was necessary to take *Elysia* into dry dock after we had discharged our Bombay cargo. Once in the dry dock, the source of the leak was identified and repaired with a steel plate welded over the damage. Other work included repairs to the rudder, chipping the rust off the underwater hull and painting the ship's bottom. During the removal of rust, one of the workers put his chipping hammer through the side of the ship where the hull was little thicker than paper! In hindsight this might have been expected as *Elysia* was over 30 years old, and but for the onset of war would by now have been withdrawn from service. Because there remained cargo for the coastal ports on the inner side of the new hole, the repair could only be made after this cargo had been discharged. Therefore we had to move out of the dry dock, discharge the coastal cargo into barges, and then re-enter the dry dock for the repair. I was very annoyed because this delayed my seeing Janet. The dry dock gave us apprentices the chance to study the underwater parts of *Elysia*. One day the Captain joined us to discuss what we saw.

Throughout our stay in Bombay we suffered from the hottest weather of the year. At dances, my shirt and jacket were soaked in sweat after an hour. It was very uncomfortable, but everyone was in the same state. One night I called Angus, one of the quartermasters, to go on gangway watch. Even after I shook him he showed no signs of life and, worried, I woke the ship's doctor. After examining Angus, the doctor concluded it was probably a case of exhaustion caused by the heat or sunstroke, and he prescribed cold water and a fan. I got these things and, using a damp towel, kept Angus's head cool and from time to time poured cold water on his chest. Someone had to stay up with Angus all night, so I took the job and passed the time reading and writing and every hour or so going along for a cup of tea. Initially Angus was very restless, but later he fell into a deep sleep. After a day he recovered.

One morning when we got up we found a wind howling across the docks, sweeping sheets of torrential rain. Cargo work was out of the question, and for the first hour we were busy securing hatches and lashing down anything likely to come adrift. The water in the dock had been whipped into small waves that threatened to swamp some coal barges near us. Outside a tremendous sea was running, and every now and again a dhow broke adrift and was driven ashore. A boom defence ship was dragging her anchors but managed to get into the lee of a small island. By noon, the worst of the cyclone had passed so that we were able to resume cargo in the afternoon. We learned that the storm had caused widespread damage.

In our spare time we engaged in a variety of activities. During the lunch hour stoppage of cargo work, our soccer team practised on a space behind the cargo sheds. We had a match against a large armed merchant cruiser. We were fortunate in having some very good players and won by one goal to nil. By the end of the game we were all slowed down by the heat. Afterwards our opponents came back to *Elysia* for some beer. Dougie gave us money and the afternoon off to go to our favourite swimming place, Breach Candy. Another day when we were free we went to the Tower of Silence, where the Parsis customarily left their dead in the open. Our guide told us that they did so in order not to defile (by cremating or burying the corpses or putting them in the water) the air, earth and water that they believe were sacred. Because only officials were allowed inside the towers, the guide showed us a model. The three high walls formed three concentric circles with a well in the centre. Each circle was divided into numerous, shallow coffins with the outer ring for males, the next ring for females and the inner one for children. When a body was brought to the Tower, the attendants carried it on an iron stretcher and placed it in one of the open coffins. There it was left exposed to the sun, and the vultures that perched on the surrounding trees served to remove the flesh. The bones were turned into dust by the heat of the sun, and when the rains came they were washed down the well, back into the earth again.

With all the delays to *Elysia*, it was 23 days before we were ready to sail, bound for the coastal ports and Karachi. I had never been so glad to see the last of Bombay with its heat and mosquitoes. In my eagerness to get to Karachi, time seemed to drag. When we finally arrived after a six-day passage there was a note from Janet asking me to phone her. We arranged to meet at the entrance to the docks at 4.30 p.m. Time dragged interminably until it was time to go ashore and meet her. Having imagined her so often, I wondered whether my picture of her had become a little distorted since I had last seen her nearly a year ago, but she was still as beautiful. We drove in her car to her home, and entering her front gate was like passing from India back to England. The desert sand and dust were shut out, replaced by a tree-shaded green lawn, high hedges of evergreens, flowers, and a pergola with wicker chairs and a table spread for tea. Mrs Mackay came to meet us. She was charming, courteous, and devoid of that snobbery that I had noticed in so many British people who lived in India. She was a good conversationalist, who quickly put me at ease. After tea, Janet and I went for a walk. We had plenty to talk about, and I felt as if we could have gone on for hours. Janet told me something of the life and people she had met in India, and about the European habit of heavy drinking, which she disliked.

Returning to the ship, I learned that *Elysia* was to be shifted across to a different dock next evening. After taking several hours to summon up courage, I asked Dougie whether I could be ashore during the shift. He had no objection, but the Captain was in a bad mood and might not like it. During a long silence while Dougie sat thinking I was on tenterhooks, deciding that, if necessary, I would go the Old Man myself. However, Dougie finally said, "Well, you will be away before he finds out anyhow." It was very good of him. Again the day dragged interminably. At lunchtime I phoned Janet to say I was free, and she promised to meet me.

I slipped ashore, fearing that Dougie might change his mind. When Janet arrived we drove back to the house, where we had tea out in the garden with Commander and Mrs Mackay. I had not been sure what to make of Janet's father, but tonight I saw that under a rather gruff exterior he was kind-hearted man with a sense of humour and a keen mind. As soon as tea was finished, he left for golf. Mrs Mackay, Janet and I decided to go to the zoo. Janet and I wandered round, talking like old friends. It seemed hard to believe that we had only met on shore for the first time yesterday. After a while, we rejoined Mrs Mackay at the car and drove back to their house. The road wound among low sand hills on which grew thickets of cacti. It was like the country one sees in wild west films, and only needed a stagecoach being held up by mounted bandits to complete the picture.

When we got back, we sat talking for a while before Janet suggested taking the dog for a walk. It was quite cold and Janet put on my sports jacket. There was great happiness in being alone together in the moonlight, which seemed to make the world recede and leave us alone with the darkness and the stars. At first conversation seemed difficult, but soon we were talking freely. She told me that the object of most girls in coming to India was to find a husband, and she disliked the way people thrust young men at her to their mutual embarrassment. It was rather like a mannequin parade for the purpose of buying a frock. Her purpose in coming to India was to be with her parents. Janet wanted to make her own friends, and hoped that she might remain as natural and unspoiled by India as her mother. I told her about my family, of what I hoped to do, and the probable difficulties of earning a living when the war was over. As we left this world of stars and darkness, we stopped to look back, and then kissed before returning to the house. During the evening, I was made to feel very much at home. Shortly after 10 they drove me back to the ship.

The following day while on cargo work, and not busy going round the hatches, I watched the big ocean-going dhows entering and leaving port. There was no wind, and the boats they carried were out ahead towing with up to 20 men at the oars, rowing a quick jerky stroke with long pauses before letting the oars enter the water again. Most of the men rowed in silence, but some sang, led by the helmsman who did the solos. The Mackays had invited the Third Engineer, the Third Mate, Sparks and me to tea. We sat talking until nearly eight, when we had to leave as Sparks had an engagement. I did not enjoy the evening much as it was hard to make polite conversation when I would have liked to have Janet to myself. The previous night, when Janet and I came in from our walk, I noticed her mother give her a quick, shrewd glance. I think she knew what was going on.

Next day the loading of cargo would be complete, and we were scheduled to leave on the following day. At lunchtime I phoned Janet to ask if I could see her again in the evening. She said she would be playing tennis early, but if I could find my way to her house she would be home by eight o'clock. During the afternoon I felt rotten, realizing how terribly pushy I must seem practically asking myself out. But I wouldn't see Janet again for ages, maybe never. To get to the Mackays' I took a tram part way and then had a half-hour's walk. As I approached her house, I could see into the lighted sitting room where Janet, who had been knitting, stood up on hearing my footsteps. She met me on the veranda and we went back into the sitting room. A few minutes later Commander and Mrs Mackay joined us. I had wondered whether they would show any signs of annoyance at my being so forward, but they welcomed me warmly. Again we had an enjoyable evening, talking on a variety of subjects. After dinner Janet showed me how to play mah-jong. Apart from the pleasure of being instructed by Janet, it was a joy simply to listen to her voice, which was soft and musical. Just before 10.30 p.m. the Mackays said they would take me back to the ship, and while they were putting on more clothes – the nights were beginning to get chilly – I saw Janet alone for a few moments and asked her whether I might have some photos of her. She had no time to find them but promised to post them. Driving back in the car we spoke little. There was so much I would have liked to say but was unable to, although I was sure she understood.

At length we reached the docks, the car stopped, and I had to leave my seat beside Janet. I said goodbye and thanked the Mackays for their hospitality and kindness. Some day I hoped I might be able to repay some of this kindness. I did not wait to see the car drive off but walked slowly back to the ship. The few days that I had waited so impatiently for were over. I lay awake for hours thinking of all the incidents of the past few days

We sailed at 3 p.m. next day. It was not until the Pilot had left and the white foaming wake lengthened between the ship and Karachi that I felt utterly wretched and was ashamed of having to stop myself from crying. For the remainder of the evening I felt a dull, aching pain in my stomach and could think of no one but Janet. It was useless dreaming of what was past, and I resolved to look ahead, work for the future, and stop my thoughts from wandering.

We were going directly to Cape Town without stopping at Bombay. Two days out from Karachi the rain started with increasingly severe squalls. During the evening watch the storm became severe, and I was glad to turn in at midnight even though my bunk was wet from a wave coming through my less than perfect "watertight" porthole. I had just managed to get to sleep when Marshall, the apprentice, woke me and told me to come and help swing in the lifeboats. I slipped on a pair of shorts and a shirt and hurried up to the boat deck where all the deck hands were turning to. The lifeboats were kept swung out ready to lower quickly in case an enemy attack led to our having to abandon ship. The storm had become so violent that there was a danger of their being smashed by the waves. Our task was to swing them inboard and secure them before they were stove in by the heavy rolling of the ship. The Captain had hove to the ship to make her ride more easily, in order to make our work easier. Once a boat was ready to swing in, I climbed up one of the two davits used for swinging the boat inboard and lowered myself into the boat. A sailor followed me to help, and we passed out to the men on deck the ropes to the blocks and tackles that raised or lowered the lifeboats (the fall ropes).

It was exciting work climbing about in the darkness with the angry sea 40 feet below. While the boat was being swung in, the sailor and I had to sit down, generally in a pool of water. We were soaked to the skin, and grew very cold. It looked a strange, wild world up on the boat deck. Above the roar of the wind I could just hear the shouted orders of the mates and the Serang, and the monotonous chorus of the men as they heaved on the falls. The darkness was full of shapes and figures, and the mates' torches flittingly lit up the faces of the men working. There was no way to measure time in that angry howling world, and when the boats were secured I slipped down for some tea. Feeling wet and cold, I turned in around 3 a.m. but did not sleep well because of the noise of the storm and the leak in my porthole. By morning the worst of the cyclone had passed and we resumed our course.

On the long passage to Cape Town there was plenty of time to read, and with my vivid memories of Janet it was perhaps natural that I should choose *Romeo and Juliet*. The following passage struck me especially:

> ROMEO: How sweet is love itself possess'd,
> When but love's shadows are so rich in joy.

But Friar Lawrence replies:

> These violent delights have violent ends,
> And in their triumph die; like fire and powder
> Which as they kiss, consume; the sweetest honey
> Is loathsome in his own deliciousness
> And in the taste compounds the appetite
> Therefore, love moderately; long love doth so;
> Too swift arrives as tardy as too slow.

Somehow I found these lines comforting.

After a 20-day passage we reached Cape Town. This time I was able to go ashore, and during our short stay I bought 10 pounds of butter for the Chief Officer and 5 pounds for my family that I stored in the ship's refrigerator to supplement the meagre rations then in force in Britain.

On previous visits I had looked longingly at Table Mountain as one I would like to climb. While ashore I made enquiries about routes up the mountain and determined to try to climb it next morning between four and eight o'clock when I was off watch. There were two Royal Indian Navy Cadets passengers whom I persuaded to join me on the expedition.

We left in the dark shortly after 4 a.m., taking some sandwiches and chocolate. In less than an hour we reached Klook Nak, which is a dip in the hills between the Lion's Head Mount and Table Mount. Continuing, we met some road menders who put us onto a track that spiralled steeply upwards among the trees. Coming to a fork, we took the left-hand turn that we soon realized was leading us up the Devil's Peak. We climbed above the tree line, still among flowers; then the path led us along narrow ledges high up on the faces of precipices. It was wild and lovely as we zigzagged upwards, and the mountain air, the early morning, the exercise and the enjoyment of being up on the mountains again made me feel happier and more uplifted than I had felt since leaving Karachi.

On a peak above us we sighted a small hut. As the path went close by it we crossed over, and we met a firewatcher. It was a perfect position for him because the forests, Cape Town and Table Bay lay below us, and we stopped for a while to admire the glorious view. Then, having little time left, we pushed on up to the mist level, where we finally halted beside a big rock and a small clump of pines. Here we were several hundred feet above the Lion's Head. I hated to turn back, but our time was running out and were were putting to sea at 10 a.m. That evening, after my watch, my legs were so tired that I could not lift them to untie my shoelaces.

While at Cape Town we apprentices bought a small bottle of ketchup. Although there was a good stock of tomato ketchup in the ship's stores, the Chief Steward had not let us have any at meals and this annoyed us. To get our own back on the Chief Steward, we took the bottle we had bought into meals. To the growing amazement of the stewards, the amount of ketchup in the bottle remained the same day after day. Marshall, on his 12 to 4 night watch, had found where the Steward kept the ketchup and each night replenished our bottle.

One day the Third Mate produced a cricket bat that someone had found. We made a ball out of rags, and a craze for cricket started. Unfortunately it was only too easy to hit a ball overboard. It would have been easy to rig a preventive net; however, it was of no use to ask Dougie because he disliked our playing games, so we kept losing rag balls and had to make new ones.

As I was nearing the end of my apprenticeship, I spent more time in studying for the Second Mate's exams. A difficult part of the exams was the 31 articles of the rules of the road at sea. To satisfy examiners in the oral exam they gave on the articles, the candidate was expected to have memorized the articles and to thoroughly understand their meaning. I had difficulty memorizing, so I wrote each article on a card and if things were quiet when I was on watch I used the cards as an aid to learning. Off watch, I would find someone who would listen to what I had learned and would correct me if I made a mistake or could not remember.

While at sea I read a book called *Jonathan North* and I identified with one of the characters, Francis, who was a pacifist. In a talk with his father, he defends his principles that war never justifies the ends claimed for it but is always evil. He tells his father that he would never participate in a war. His father replies, "If war comes, whether our case is good or only middling, nearly all the folk you like from the best as well as the worst off will fight. And when you see 'em doing it, getting killed and wounded for what they think is right--you won't be able to stand it--not for long. You'll go and join in. That's what happened last time and what'll always happen." His son replies, "That would be the worst of all, to be fighting, knowing in your heart you are wrong to do it."

The conversation interested me intensely, as the question had been troubling me since the outbreak of war. I agreed with all Francis said, but ever since the gun was mounted on *Elysia* I had been retreating step by step from the principles that Christ outlined in the Sermon on the Mount. I had noticed that many of my friends who had been pacifists had also done so. Why was this? Is it that we were afraid of public opinion? That we realized the futility of trying to dissociate ourselves from the war, owing to the present organization of the country? That the public press had managed to convince us that we were fighting for a worthwhile purpose? That we had become infected with the war fever that had spread throughout the country like a plague? Even Daddy, who had several times made great sacrifices for his pacifist views, told me when I was home that he could no longer call himself a hard-boiled pacifist! It may be that my retreat had been due to passing through the youthful idealistic period and finding that these ideals would not fit into the world of today. Is this what Wordsworth meant when he wrote these lines?

> The youth who daily farther from the East
> Must travel, still is Nature's priest,
> And by the vision splendid
> Is on his way attended.
> At length the man perceives it die away
> And fade into the light of common day!

Looked at from a distance, one could easily form an opinion about war: that the enemy stood for everything that was degrading, false and evil, and that we were defending justice, freedom, liberty of speech and all the principles that a democratic nation holds dear. Or, as a clergyman might put it, "We were fighting the powers of darkness with the sword of righteousness." If all this were true, our course of action would be obvious; but when we come closer to the picture, these noble sentiments no longer appear so substantial or gilded. We see two nations at war, each employing its entire resources in the attempt to conquer the other, each believing they are in the right, making tremendous sacrifices, and in doing so jeopardizing their own and their children's lives and future happiness. We see millions of people without any personal cause for hatred, who only ask to be allowed to carry on their lives in peace, leaving their work, friends and families and after a short course of training in the butchery of their fellow men going out to put that training into practice. The deeper we look, the less sincere the first picture we were shown appears. We become troubled and perplexed, not knowing what to think or do. There being no apparent answer, we cease to think, stand back from the picture of war again, and find that unless we want to be very awkward we just do as we are told by the government of the country.

After leaving Cape Town the Captain ordered that the entire ship's company was to be trained in air raid precautions. They had to be able to use the equipment we had on board to fight fires, to always have their gas masks handy and know how to use them, to know the safest places to be during an air raid, and so on. The task of training fell to the Third Mate and me. Every afternoon we took groups from the crew until they were all trained. We had difficulty instructing some of the Indian sailors and firemen because our Hindustani was sadly limited and it was next to impossible for them to imagine what an actual bomb was like.

On 9 December we reached Freetown, where we stayed for five days waiting for enough ships to make up a convoy. The Commodore again chose to sail with his staff on our ship. While at Freetown I received a letter from Mother, who wrote that someone had told her he had seen a notice that the time period required to make apprentices eligible to sit for their Second Mate's certificates had been shortened from four to three years. The decision had been made because so many merchant seamen officers had been lost through enemy action. The news excited me tremendously because it meant that this would be my last voyage as an apprentice. It would mean a spell at home, passing my exams, a change of ship and a decent wage as Third Mate. I would be terribly disappointed if there had been some mistake and it was a false alarm.

Sometimes I wondered why I spent so long studying. At times it seemed like a drug to keep my mind occupied. Whenever my mind wandered it was away from the ship, either to my home life or to memories of happy times spent with friends and Janet. Being here seemed like being on a bridge between my hopes for the future and memories of the past. Did studying only strengthen the gate closing me off from the world I wished to live in? It seemed an unnatural life that shut me off from the company, recreation and activities that made life worth living. Perhaps a good reason for studying was that it kept my brain active in readiness for any opportunity that might crop up for a change of vocation.

On 15 December we weighed anchor with the Commodore and his staff aboard, and led the convoy of 25 ships out from the harbour, escorted by two armed trawlers that stayed with us for two weeks. One evening we saw what looked like a white flare being sent up. Because the signal meant that a submarine had been sighted, or a ship torpedoed, we called the Commodore, but nothing materialized. Two days later a ship in the convoy signalled sighting a submarine. Again nothing happened. With so many lookouts on the ships searching the sea for signs of a periscope, any disturbance of the sea surface could seem to be a periscope. So we had to expect a number of false alarms, but each alarm had to be taken seriously. When submarines attacked by day they would try to manoeuvre in front of the convoy and remain stationary, only briefly raising their periscopes for a look round. Then they would wait until the convoy was passing them, and fire their torpedoes. Submerging, they would risk being sunk by depth charges. At night when it was very difficult to see them they approached on the surface. They would come in close on the beam, fire their torpedoes and beat a hasty retreat at full speed (about 18 knots).

The trawler escort left before we were scheduled to meet the larger escort that would take us through the Western Approaches to Britain. For two days we had no escort and everyone was deeply concerned until our new escort showed up, consisting of an armed merchant cruiser, a destroyer, a corvette and several armed trawlers. That evening some parachute flares were dropped from allied aircraft in an attempt to spot a submarine suspected of being in the vicinity. The Commodore altered the course of the convoy, and shortly afterwards we heard depth charges. The Captain asked passengers to volunteer for lookout duty, and seven or eight were on duty at all times, including our officers, who were put on double watches. Approaching England we became very restive, and to keep us occupied in our spare time the game of Monopoly became popular, and although it was very cold several of us took up cricket again, wearing heavy sweaters and gloves with the fingers cut off.

On Christmas Day nothing was done to celebrate. It had been this way on previous Christmases on *Elysia*. I was terribly disappointed by the way in which no one gave consideration to the happiness of the crew or troubled to take any steps to give us a good time. I tried to follow the hard saying "Blessed is he that expecteth nothing; for he shall not be disappointed". It was as well I did, because apart from an improvement of the menus and decorations hung in the saloon, nothing out of the ordinary happened. We could have had dinner with the passengers, but the purser would not take the trouble to make the arrangements. A cynical mind would have found our Christmas dinner a humorous sight. Four groups were seated well apart from one another: Three DBS (Distressed British Seamen travelling as passengers), the Commodore's staff, the children and their mothers and we three apprentices. Such an arrangement made the decorations appear a mockery. I should have been thankful for the good food, a bunk to sleep in and the fact that we were still afloat. How many millions were spending this Christmas Day with no coal for their fires, wondering where their next meal would come from? It was the loneliness that I felt most, and the way in which the people who could have brought us together made no effort to do so.

During the evening watch on New Year's Eve, it was so cold that on watch I wore pyjama trousers under my uniform and a balaclava helmet. At midnight we all wished each other a happy New Year, and when I came down from the bridge I found a party had started in the Carpenter's cabin. Some of the quartermasters, a passenger and much whisky, beer and cigarettes were present. The talk and song became more voluble and less intelligent as time went on. Most of them sang, and I took my turn. I left soon after, since I was sleepy and the thick tobacco smoke stung my eyes. Afterwards I learned that some at the party got drunk. At any time at sea this would have been a foolish thing to do, but under the constant threat of attack it was criminal. In an emergency they could have let down people who depended on them for their safety.

On 3 January we sighted the Scottish lighthouse Innistrahul, and as the daylight grew stronger we could make out the welcome sight of the Western Highlands with Jura, Islay and the Mull of Kintyre. The mountains covered with snow looked lovely. The day passed quickly, with my spare time taken up with writing letters and plenty to do on watch as we were coming down the Irish Sea between England and Ireland. Next morning we picked up a Liverpool pilot. Coming up the channel to Liverpool, we saw the masts of sunken ships and learned from the Pilot that they were victims of the new Vibretic mine that was detonated by the vibration of a ship passing over it. They were dropped from planes, with parachutes attached. Off the docks were two wrecks, one of which was bombed during a tremendous air raid at Christmas time, when hundreds of planes took part and thousands of people were killed.

We anchored in the early afternoon. Soon afterwards a tender came alongside to take off the passengers and their baggage. The mail was given out, but to our disappointment much of it must have been adrift as most of the letters were old and many that were expected did not arrive. I took the opportunity to send a telegram with one of the Commodore's signalmen to let my parents know we had arrived safely.

About 4 p.m., we went to "stations" for docking; after several delays we were finally taken just inside the docks and tied up for the night. By this time it was dark and bitterly cold, with a thick fog. Next morning we were meant to have moved to our berth in the docks, but no movement of ships was allowed as officials were attempting to remove an unexploded time bomb on the docks. At last we got under way, but it was nearly 4 p.m.

before we finally reached the berth where we would discharge our cargo. The damage done to the docks during the "blitz" was appalling, with sheds that contained valuable cargoes gutted, many ships badly damaged as a result of the bombing, and buildings blackened by fires. The world must have gone crazy to allow such ruthless and useless destruction. After tea, several of us went for a short walk and everywhere saw broken windows, gaunt skeletons of bombed warehouses silhouetted against the moonlit clouds and in one place a huge crater in the road.

I was in Liverpool for the next 10 days, and tried to record some of the differences I found since we were here last. Streets were crowded with people, many in uniform and few looking as though they had time to waste. The shops had broken windows replaced by wooden boarding with a small glass observation panel left in the centre. Prices were noticeably higher and fashions conformed to the times, being designed for warmth and utility rather than catching the eye. At the bus and tram stops there were generally small crowds waiting for transport. People wanted to get home before the blackout to avoid being delayed by the air raid sirens' mournful wail. I felt so sorry for the small shopkeepers, who through restriction on supplies had to turn away customers.

In poor neighbourhoods near the docks, long blocks of houses had ragged holes torn in them by high explosive bombs. Among the piles of rubble, charred wood and twisted beams, odds and ends stood out pathetic and untouched: a picture on a scarred wall, a small table or a broken doll. Yet less than a stone's throw away, shops still carried on. Some had their whole fronts shattered and many of their wares spoiled, yet up went any old board for repair with notices scrawled on them in chalk such as: "Business as usual, we hope. The blasted window has gone, but we are still here." No wonder Germany had failed to break the morale of these people.

Looking at the changes from a purely selfish point of view, we found that entertainments were more difficult to get to. The last showing of the pictures started at 6 p.m., and afterwards we had the blackout and sometimes rotten weather to contend with on our way back to *Elysia*. A fine evening generally brought over the enemy planes, and this meant possibly hours of standing in shelters and a long walk home, since all public services stopped running as soon as the gunfire started.

I learned that the information Mother had sent me in a letter was true. The sea time required for sitting the Second Mate's exams had been reduced from four years to three. I obtained leave from the Anchor Line to prepare for and take the exams. On 17 January 1941 I left *Elysia* and after a week's holiday started studying at the Glasgow Technical College. I lived at my parents' home in Paisley and used my bicycle to travel the eight miles to the college. After eight weeks of study I took, and passed, the exams. My parents shared with me in my delight at the result, and I had some quiet days of rest at home. I was happy to see that my father got back the £25 that he had paid to the Anchor Line at the start of my apprenticeship, plus interest.

CHAPTER 2

Empire Beaver

Voyage 1 – April to July 1941

When I reported the exam result to the Anchor Line they offered me a berth as Third Mate on a cargo ship, the *Empire Beaver*, and the Marine Superintendent took me down to see the ship. He told me she had been built in the United States, and after many years of service had been transferred to the British as part of the Lend Lease programme. Her next voyage was to New York, and her Master was Captain Johnson, with whom I had sailed on *Elysia* and whom I liked.

When we boarded the ship, my impression was far from good as she looked like an old tramp steamer. The ship's company was having dinner when we entered the saloon, and with them was Mr MacGilvray, the Chief Officer from the *Elysia*. He congratulated me on getting my ticket, introduced me to some of the officers, and asked me to stay to dinner. He urged me to take the berth, and since I took a liking to the people I saw and wanted to see New York, I accepted the job. For a while I had been feeling restless, knowing that I could be of some use at sea but of no use at home. The pay would be £24 ($96) a month, a 12-fold increase over what I received during my last year as an apprentice.

Empire Beaver was sailing in two days, and I had to rush to collect my gear and get it aboard, sign on the ship's articles and say goodbye to my family and friends. I did take time to buy enough gold braid to make a single stripe on each of the lower ends of my uniform sleeves as the insignia of my status of Third Mate. Later when on the ship, I sewed on the stripes.

The Second Mate, James Anderson (Wee Jimmy), took me around the ship. It was better prepared for war than the *Elysia*, with life rafts as well as lifeboats, anti-aircraft guns, a surface gun and army gunners aboard. I turned in fairly early but my mind was racing, thinking about the ship, the new work and a hundred other things. I lay awake for hours, only occasionally dozing off into a troubled sleep.

Next morning, 19 April, all hands were called at five; I went up to the bridge to see whether everything was in order for sailing. The ship had been considerably damaged by a blast in the heavy air raids on the docks, and the bridge was covered with odds and ends left over from hastily done repairs. I had started cleaning up when the Old Man and the Second Mate joined in the work. By the time we left at 6 a.m. things were comparatively tidy. After the *Elysia*, with her four quartermasters, three apprentices and numerous Indian sailors and stewards, this ship seemed terribly shorthanded, and I realized that I would have more work to do than a Third Mate on *Elysia*.

On our way down the river it started to rain hard. With the cold east wind it was most unpleasant, as we had an open bridge. By lunchtime we were anchored. During the afternoon I tidied up my cabin, which was far larger and more comfortable than my last, the greatest luxuries being a washbasin with hot and cold running water and a good writing table. The food was very good. After the rationing of meat, cheese, eggs, butter and other foods at home, here we had all we could want.

During the evening I got to know some of the ship's company. Wee Jimmy was a small, cheery person, easy to get on with and very intelligent. The Senior Sparks (one of our two wireless operators) affected a rather military manner, possibly imitating his family who were all in the army. Once I got over this manner I found him friendly and good company.

During the two days we spent at anchor in the Firth of Clyde, I had an opportunity to settle down and get to know the ropes. There was a great deal of work to do getting the ship ready to go to sea: putting the lifeboats, rafts and fire fighting appliances in good order, correcting books on convoy signals, checking boat and fire stations, and learning where the ship's gear was kept and about the guns installed for our defence.

One afternoon there was an air raid warning and everyone went to action stations, but we only heard planes and it became a chance for a pleasant talk with Captain Johnson on the bridge. On *Elysia* all anchor watches were kept on the bridge, but here we worked on deck during the day watches. During the night watches I remained in my cabin as long as the ship was riding easily, leaving word with the night watchman to call to me if I was wanted. Every now and again I took a stroll around to see that everything was all right. On Tuesday morning the new Mate, Mr Jenkins, came aboard and our first impression of him was not good. (On cargo ships the term Mate, or First Mate, rather than Chief Officer was generally used.) He resembled Winston Churchill, except that his face was fatter and very red, and his eyes were more sunken; he looked like a heavy drinker. His uniform was very shabby. However, we learned he was a seaman of the old school, whose whole life and interests centred on ships, and who was kind-hearted, considerate and easy to work with.

Glasgow to New York

On Tuesday evening we were scheduled to put to sea at midnight. Because a strong east wind had sprung up and a ship was lying close to windward, I spent the evening watch on the lower bridge revising convoy instructions and watching to see that the ship ahead did not drag her anchor. When the time came, I called all hands needed for getting under way. Shortly before midnight we weighed anchor and proceeded in pitch darkness out through the gate in the boom defence. (In harbours where ships gathered, a wire net was stretched from shore to shore to keep out German submarines. The gate in the boom was opened when Allied ships entered or left.)

Next morning we joined the main convoy from Liverpool, and for the next five days were very lucky considering that we were in the main danger zone of the Western Approaches. This area was north, west and south of Ireland, where merchant shipping converged en route for the western ports of the United Kingdom. Because of this it was a favourite hunting ground for German submarines at this period of the war. Our convoy, steaming slowly at six to seven knots, had a good escort of destroyers, sloops, corvettes and trawlers, and some aircraft circled overhead. On watch there was plenty to do: maintaining our correct station in the convoy, hoisting and reading flag signals, and taking bearings to fix our position. It was a great pleasure being in charge of the watch and making all the decisions myself instead of always having to ask permission before taking any action. The 8 to 12 evening watch seemed very long, now that I could not get off the bridge for supper at 10. One of the wireless operators who was on watch with me to help with the signalling brought me a plate of sandwiches and some cocoa. During an evening watch, a destroyer just ahead of us dropped four depth charges but no developments followed. At sea these days it was foolish to undress at night because we might be called out at any time for an emergency, so in order to get a change of clothes I changed into pyjamas and over them pulled on a jersey and an old pair of trousers. Up on the bridge, in addition to carrying a torch and a knife on a belt under my coat, I had a whistle, a life jacket with an electric life light attached, and a steel helmet in case of sudden air attack.

Sometimes the Old Man would join me on the bridge, and when all was quiet we would talk. He told me what he thought about the poor way the Anchor Line Glasgow office people acted: we need not have left Glasgow for another two days, but they were so afraid the crew would desert that they sent us down the Clyde on Saturday. The ship was badly in need of a dry docking and many other repairs, but the authorities didn't think it worth spending money on a ship that could be a total loss any day. He felt that all the office cared about was getting the ships off their hands and out to sea again as quickly as possible, irrespective of their condition and the safety of the ship and her crew. They primarily wanted to please the Ministry of Shipping. Then he said that going to sea was a fool's game. Later, as I got to know him better, I found that he had a vein of bitterness and cynicism that I think was due to the conditions under which he had had to work, and to slow promotion. Several times his hopes of being made Master were frustrated, although from all I had heard and seen of him he was a conscientious worker and highly efficient. I tended to agree with much that he said. He knew his crew but seemed to emphasize their bad side. He treated them well but seemed to lack the diplomacy necessary for getting the best out of them. I preferred a more tactful approach.

After five days at sea, the convoy dispersed. With all the extra work needed on watch while we were in convoy, I still had time to take sights with my sextant and fix the ship's position. During the day watches I had opportunities to talk to the army gunners, who manned the anti-aircraft gun and now kept daylight lookouts on the bridge. Only the corporal in charge was in the regular army. The others were drawn from various jobs: one was a mechanic in a large factory, another a salesman of fabrics, and a third combined professional football and coach work at Morris Motors. The Captain appointed me gunnery officer for the ship, responsible to him for seeing that the gun crews were trained, the armament was in good condition and the ammunition in order, and also to act as control officer for the 4.7-inch gun. Five years previously I could not have believed that I would be in this position on board a ship whose main cargo was whisky, beer and materials for munitions.

I found that there were advantages in being on a cargo ship with no passengers. It was a relief not to have to worry about their safety in the event that the ship was sunk. As one of the mates on *Elysia* had said, "Passengers are the most troublesome form of cargo." On the *Beaver* life was more informal. We did not have to wear uniform and could dress as we liked. We had the run of the ship without being restricted by spaces reserved for passengers. Because we had an all British crew, communication between officers and the rest of the crew was not constrained by different languages and cultures

The engineers found that all the oil fuel tanks had been polluted with water. On three occasions during our passage to New York the *Empire Beaver* had to be stopped for several hours while repairs were carried out. Black smoke belched out of the funnel, giving away our position to distant ships that might include German submarines or raiders. Each time we were glad to get under way again, as it was no place in which to hang around.

We encountered two storms that slowed our passage. One evening's watch was to be the toughest I had yet experienced. The wind seemed determined to tear the ship to pieces. Squalls screamed by, making it difficult to stand still without holding onto something for support. Sheets of torrential rain battered against the canvas dodgers that were meant to give us some protection from the elements, and drove into the sea with a sullen hiss that could just be heard during lulls in the gale. For the first hours of the watch, blinding flashes of lightning followed each other in rapid succession and rumbles of thunder rolled across the sky. How puny all man's devices of war seemed beside nature's wrath. Towards midnight the rainsqualls came less often and a few stars broke through the ragged flying clouds. When I went up to the bridge next morning, I thought that the storm must have been a dream. A pleasant gentle breeze cooled me from the hot sun, and only a slight swell was left to make the *Beaver* roll easily. The morning passed enjoyably as I took sights and worked out our position.

For some time, the Mate had suspected that the whisky in the holds was being pilfered. One morning he was proved right, as several of the sailors were so drunk that they were unfit for duty. The Mate and Jimmy searched aft and found several bottles hidden away. After lunch, Jimmy and I searched the crew's quarters and, stashed in a spare ventilator, I found a case with five bottles. The Captain set a guard on the after deck to see that nothing more was stolen.

At New York

On 12 May, after a slow passage of 21 days from Scotland, we passed the Ambrose Light, which marks the entrance to New York harbour, and took on the Pilot. We anchored off Staten Island at the quarantine station, and for several hours the saloon was filled with medical, immigration and customs officials. All the crew had their fingerprints taken and we were given alien registration receipt cards in place of our identity cards, which were kept by the shore authorities until we sailed. We then proceeded past the Statue of Liberty and the view of the Manhattan skyline and went on to dock at a pier in Brooklyn.

As the danger of sabotage to ships in port was considerable, we had to take numerous precautions. Shore guards were on duty day and night and our soldiers guarded the guns. At night the ship was brilliantly lit. A ship's officer had to be dressed and awake all night. For the first few days we were on duty about nine hours a day. Then the First Mate lost control and for several days drank so much that he was useless and a thorough nuisance. On 21 May we shifted into Erie Basin preparatory to entering the dry dock, and I had my first experience of being in charge aft. I made several mistakes, and afterwards the Old Man gave me valuable advice about what I had forgotten to do and how it should be done. The same day the Mate was taken to hospital because he was severely drunk; this left Jimmy and me with all his work to do in addition to our own. To relieve this stress the Old Man paid Senior Sparks overtime to be on duty every second night. I had to take the other nights, and Jimmy was on during the day.

We were in dry dock for only two days, but as there was a great deal of work remaining to be done in the engine room and fuel tanks we remained at the repair dock for several further days. Sometimes I was the only mate on duty and the Old Man would give me a list of work he wanted done. It was difficult keeping an eye on everything going on, but it was also good fun and I was learning a great deal. The Bosun knew his work thoroughly and was reliable, but he did not have the gift of running the crew. He tended to do a job on his own and leave several of the crew looking on. On 28 May we shifted across to Pier 7, Jersey City, and commenced loading scrap iron, but the work was stopped after we found that two plates in the hull at No. 1 hold were cracked and leaking badly. The surveyor was called; he decided that doubling plates must be welded on. More cargo was loaded in the stern to tip the bow out of the water so that the repair work could be performed. After the repair to the cracked plates was completed the loading of scrap continued, only to be abruptly stopped when it was discovered that the soundings of No. 1 bilge showed a steady increase in the depth of water. A Lloyd's surveyor and other officials came down, but as soon as they arrived no more water entered the bilge! For the next few days the bilge sometimes indicated a leak and at other times did not. No one could explain the mystery, and as there were not sufficient grounds to warrant sending the ship back to the dry dock, the loading was resumed.

During our stay in New York, five sailors and a fireman deserted out of our crew of 30 men. The temptation to desert was great, as American ships were very short of crews and wages were three or four times more than could be earned on a British ship. It was suspected that German agents were giving every aid to deserters in order to delay British ships. Another source of trouble and anxiety was the slack way in which our gunners kept watch at the guns. They grumbled a great deal because they did not think it was their place to keep night watches, even though they were only on watch for two to four hours each day. On night duty, the Second Mate, Sparks and I had the rotten task of trying to keep them at their posts and reporting them to the Old Man if they fell asleep, failed to be on board to keep their watch or were drunk. The difficulty was to know how strict to be. If I was officious and forever chasing them back to their post and reporting them, I would be thoroughly disliked and get no cooperation. If I shut my eyes to all breaches of discipline, it would save me a great deal of trouble but the gun would not be watched. Having a Mate who set a bad example by being drunk, was often absent from work and gave no help did not make it any easier for us. For the last day or two he was stupid with drink, and although he was on deck trying to run the crew, he just made himself objectionable to everybody and prevented Jimmy and me from taking any men away to do work that we thought necessary.

Our 37-day stay was due to the decrepit condition of *Empire Beaver's* hull and engines, caused by her age and by neglect. This long stay gave us an extraordinary opportunity when not on duty to explore the city. On our first evening ashore, Sparks and I travelled into the heart of New York by subway. We wandered about the streets gaping at the immense electric signs, the beautifully dressed shop windows, and the endless streams of people. Several times we were nearly run over by the fast-moving traffic travelling on the right-hand side of the road, the opposite side to that used in Britain. Every time a plane passed overhead we exchanged anxious glances before remembering where we were. Even after a week's stay at New York, the wail of a particular siren momentarily scared us because it was so like an air raid warning.

I frequented the Seaman's Institute on South Street, where the staff knew what was going on in the city and gave us free passes to picture houses, theatres and concerts. The volunteers made us feel at home, and would invite us to parties, dances and visits to their homes. One of them invited me to go with her family to spend a day in the country at a cousin's home, and later I went with them to dinner and a play.

At a dance at the Overseas Club, I met Margery Hart (Midge). She had recently come from England; she was tall, and an excellent dancer. We enjoyed dancing together and found many common interests. We went to several dances, including one at Madison Square Garden, which had been transformed into the world's largest dance hall, with tropical foliage, giant palm trees, and a star-studded ceiling. Three bands, including Benny Goodman's, alternated. With some of Midge's friends, I went to the amusement park at Coney Island and had my first corn on the cob liberally covered with butter, which I found delicious. I went to several concerts, including one at the bandstand in Central Park where the music, the sunset, the ring of lights encircled by the silhouette of the trees and later a new moon sinking behind the skyscrapers made the event memorable.

I saw William MacVicar's name in a headline of a newspaper and guessed it might be my friend and former watch mate on *Elysia*. He had arrived in New York on a South American liner, after having crossed the Atlantic in a lifeboat. I found out the hotel where he was staying and went to see him. After a warm greeting he told me about the sinking of his ship, the Anchor Line *Britannia*, on which he was Third Mate. They were about 600 miles off Freetown, Sierra Leone, en route for India, with over a hundred passengers. During a morning watch, they sighted a ship with Japanese markings that then opened fire on them. The spray from the first shot soaked Mac and the second shot hit the ship. The Britannia responded with her gun, but the raider stayed out of *Britannia*'s range and kept making direct hits. After about 90 minutes the *Britannia*'s gun was silenced and Captain Colly hoisted the signal "We are going to abandon ship". The raider fired five more shots and then signalled "We will give you 20 minutes to get clear". Only four of the lifeboats had not been destroyed; MacVicar was in charge of one of them. About 80 persons crowded into his boat, leaving so little room that when Mac wanted to shift the rudder he had to unship the tiller. They watched the raider steam up close alongside the *Britannia* and pour several broadsides into her. She just crumpled up. As she took her last dive, the Captain gave three long blasts on the whistle and died with the many others for whom there were no lifeboats.

The sinking took place in the North East Trades, where the equatorial current flows west. Mac decided against trying to reach Africa because of contrary winds and currents, so set out on the 1500-mile voyage across the south Atlantic to Brazil. He told me little about the 23 days in the lifeboat that followed, but it must have been a ghastly experience. Many were wounded. Every day some people died and had to be put overboard, so the sharks followed in ever increasing numbers. I could only surmise the ordeal from some brief remarks of Mac's: he lost 36 pounds in weight, and only 38 people were still alive when they sighted land. He was too weak to walk when he got ashore, but some fishermen found him and took a note that Mac had scrawled to the nearest British Consul. The survivors were taken to a hospital where they stayed for five weeks before they were well enough to go to New York. A cable to Mac's parents in Scotland reached them four days after they had been told that he had been lost at sea. I expected a big change in him, but outwardly he seemed just the same as two years ago except that he was thinner. Our Old Man and an Anchor Line official were coming to see Mac, so regretfully I said goodbye.

New York to Sydney, Nova Scotia

We sailed on 17 June. I had had a wonderful time in New York, but the combination of my work and shore activities set a pace almost too fast for me to keep up with. I can only blame myself for missing so much sleep and not staying aboard more, but the temptation to live fully and enjoy myself while I could was too great.

On my first evening watch at sea I enjoyed the darkness, the silence, the open air and the motion of the ship after so long in a crowded city. Our passage to Sydney, Nova Scotia, in order to join a convoy was uneventful, and I used the time off watch to catch up on lost sleep, check the lifeboat gear, and give the gun crew some practice. As we came into the well-sheltered harbour of Sydney, the pitheads of the coalmines and the churches stood out from the other buildings. We steamed slowly towards our anchorage in the sparkling clear still morning, with the church bells ringing.

We spent eight days at Sydney lying at anchor waiting for a convoy. Nothing of note was happening, but I was determined to have at least one incident by which to remember my 21st birthday on 24 June so decided to go for a swim before breakfast. That morning the air and water were extremely cold, but somehow the importance of not changing my mind about the swim was great – it was rather like a test to prove I had the will power to accomplish what I set out to do. I got up quickly, went to the boat deck and dived overboard into the frigid water. I swam to the ladder with all speed, and after climbing back aboard I felt, though cold, refreshed and awake. The rest of the day was like any other at anchor: checking the lifeboats, reading, writing, listening to music on gramophone records while repairing a pair of uniform trousers, and doing odd jobs for the Old Man.

A Lieutenant O'Neal from the Naval Control Service came aboard, and hearing it was my 21st birthday invited me ashore for a swim, dinner with a Scottish family, and a dance, but the Old Man wouldn't give me shore leave. He had no objection to my going, but if he gave one person shore leave, he could not refuse others who would probably get drunk and desert. The next day at the end of taking gun drill, Jimmy came along and told me a birthday present had been brought aboard. In my cabin was a lovely birthday cake made by some of his friends and brought to the ship by Lieutenant O'Neal. It was sponge with dates in the middle, whipped cream icing and thirteen candles (all they had). I felt my thanks to Lieutenant O'Neal and his friends were totally inadequate to express how tremendously grateful I was for their kindness. At tea we lighted the candles, and then the three of us whose 21st birthdays fell in June (the Fifth Engineer, the Second Mate and I) blew out the candles and cut the cake.

Little else of note happened during the remainder of our stay. One afternoon the First Mate managed to get some whisky and became increasingly drunk. He became very rude, made spiteful and insulting remarks and generally became bestial. We were taking on fresh water from a barge, and when it left the Mate went ashore on it without permission. I did a lot of work on the lifeboats, rafts and lifebuoys and got them all in good condition for going to sea. During the evening watches I studied the revised Admiralty Merchant Shipping Instructions on how to counter new forms of hostile attacks when in convoy.

Sydney to Grangemouth, Scotland

On 1 July we set off on our travels again. We were in a long line of ships that was heading out through the gate in the boom defence along the swept channel and so to the open sea. I still found it thrilling to watch so many ships forming up into a large convoy. We were out on the port wing, a not very enviable position. During the night there was trouble with one of the boilers and we only just managed to hold the speed of the convoy.

The Commodore took the convoy far north in hopes of avoiding German submarines, and I saw the Northern Lights for the first time. The sky was a great dark blue backcloth upon which played great beams of coloured lights. They put the moonlight to shame and showed up the black silhouettes of the ships. Later we encountered a gale; seas swept across the decks of the *Beaver*, which laboured gallantly under her heavy load. The bridge was bitterly cold, swept by a strong beam wind from which it was almost impossible to shelter. I had so many clothes on that I couldn't move my arms freely and felt like a barrel. To keep my legs warm I periodically tried running on the spot, but by midnight even this did not work. Our convoy joined another convoy, and together we were over 90 ships.

Keeping station in a convoy should have been a matter of getting into our correct position and then, by trial and error, finding the number of revolutions the ship's engines should turn in order to produce the same speed as the Commodore's. In practice this didn't happen. For example, a Dutch ship ahead of us appeared to have only two speeds – very fast and very slow. One minute she would be a long way ahead of us. Then without warning she would slow down, and we would either have to follow her example or haul out to one side and let her fall astern. During the Mate's watch one morning, the Dutchman slowed down and our Mate ran up alongside and indicated quite clearly, although without speaking, what he thought of them. After that the Dutchman behaved slightly better. One of our sources of entertainment when on watch was racing the other ships at getting our hoists of flags up first after the signal went up on the commodore ship.

To make it more difficult for submarines to manoeuvre ahead of a convoy in order to get into the best position for attack, the Admiralty developed zigzagging, a procedure whereby all the ships in the convoy would at the same time alter course a specified number of degrees, either to port or to starboard. Then, after a given number of minutes, the ships would alter course a given number of degrees in the opposite direction. A number of different zigzag patterns, each lasting one hour, were given in a book on each ship. It seemed remarkable that our convoy of 90 ships could make the same alterations of course at exactly the same time. It was made possible by each ship having a special clock that could be set to ring a bell at the time of each alteration of course. The sequence of alterations was copied from the book of instructions onto a blackboard set in front of the helmsman. To execute a particular pattern of zigzagging, the Commodore would hoist a signal giving its number. Then every ship in the convoy would hoist the same signal. When the Commodore saw that all ships had received the signal and had time to make ready for the zigzag, he would lower the signal. Every ship would then do the same and the zigzag began. There was some danger in this procedure, because if some ships zigged and others zagged there could be a collision, especially if visibility was poor. With experience it was found that zigzagging was only effective for faster convoys of 12 knots or more, so it was discontinued for slow convoys because it proved to be no deterrent for submarines and increased the time for the convoy passage.

Our route took us almost as far north as Greenland and the entry of the weather in the logbook was "gentle breeze, slight sea, fine (or cloudy)". Throughout the night the northern sky never darkened, and it was as if nature had formed a perfect harmony between day and night. To the south was the deep blue sea and sky with the full moon riding majestically and serene above a path of rippling silver. It was as if nature was holding her breath at the result of her blending day and night into such artistic beauty.

Several times while we were in the Western Approaches we were called to action stations. The escorts went on submarine hunts and dropped depth charges, but we did not see the enemy. The sky was heavily overcast, making it difficult for enemy aircraft to see us. Heavy rain made us wet and miserable, but it was better than an aircraft attack.

As we entered the northern entrance to the Irish Sea we split off from the main convoy with some other ships and headed for Loch Ewe, a gathering place for convoys going round the north of Scotland to east coast ports. Our Old Man was made Commodore of this section, which meant that I had a busy and enjoyable watch making up and raising flag signal orders to our small convoy. Our escort gave us assistance, telling us anything we needed to know and leading us in towards the Loch. When we arrived a motorboat led us to our anchorage. In the dim twilight – the nearest approach to darkness they have here in summer – we could faintly see other ships at anchor, a large island in the Loch and to the east, large mountains. It was very lovely in a wild and rugged sort of way, but I was too sleepy to admire it. As soon as we anchored, I tumbled back into bed.

The early morning of 18 July was a typical morning for a Scottish loch. There was no wind, a dull leaden sky, heavy clouds brushed the hills and shut out the mountains, and a light drizzle hissed as it landed in the Loch. After breakfast patches of blue sky began to show. The Commodore of our east coast convoy weighed anchor and we straggled out after him. It became a glorious day. Some of the ships in our convoy towed balloons as a deterrent to dive bombers, and one of our escorts carried a fighter plane ready for launching by a catapult to take on enemy aircraft. While rounding the north coast of Scotland we were called to action stations several times when an air raid was in progress over Scapa Flow, the great naval base, but no aircraft came near us. The rest of the passage to Methil on the Firth of Forth was uneventful, and the glorious weather continued. We had to wait for high tide in order to get into our berth at Grangemouth.

Voyage 2 – August to November 1941

Grangemouth to Tampa, Florida

I returned to the ship after three days' leave. We had a new First Mate, Kenneth Ure, with whom I had served on *Elysia*, and a completely different set of firemen, sailors and gunners. They were much younger and a great improvement over the last crew. We saw no sign of the enemy on the passage round the north of Scotland to Loch Ewe, where we lay for three days waiting for an Atlantic convoy. These days of waiting were very welcome as there was always a tremendous amount of work that I had to do at the beginning of each voyage: making sure the lifeboat gear was in order, organizing the defences of the ship, training gun crews, checking flags and blackout, and making up lists for fire and boat stations. After we joined up with the Atlantic convoy our luck continued, with the absence of enemy action and good weather

Late at night, when things were quiet, I often had a yarn with members of the crew who kept lookout on the bridge. They would tell me about their work and their lives. One of them had a fine physique, and was fond of sports and a good boxer. I had a few rounds of sparring with him and was thankful that I have such a long reach. He made a punching bag and gave me boxing lessons. Another sailor was monkey-like in his agility and energy, and spent his spare time sketching. He has been torpedoed three times, and his ship was in Dakar when the French capitulated. According to him, when the soldiers came to take them prisoners they started clubbing the seamen and bayoneted several sailors who showed any fight. They also committed many other brutalities against defenceless men. The crew was marched ashore and put in prison for several months until, for unknown reasons, they were released.

Most of the crew had been bombed or torpedoed at least once. One of the firemen was aboard a ship that was shelled and sunk by a raider in the Indian Ocean, and many of his crew were killed. Those that got away in the lifeboats were machine gunned while trying to pick up survivors from the water. It seemed paradoxical, but once they were taken aboard the raider, they were well treated. They stayed aboard her for six weeks, until the raider commandeered a neutral Yugoslavian ship and used her as a prison ship to take the prisoners from merchant ships up to Italian Somaliland. While on this ship they were kept in the holds that were partially filled with a cargo of salt, and they nearly died of thirst. At an Italian East African port they were put in prison, joining the remnants of six other British crews. They remained there until they were liberated when the British captured the town.

The detachment of six soldiers who manned one of the anti-aircraft guns had all recently been civilians. Once we were outside the range of air attack, they acted as lookouts on the bridge. Their civilian occupations included grocer's assistant, concrete mixer, labourer, trainer of greyhounds, builder, chiropodist and librarian with a private income. The last of these was about 30 years old, and in appearance more like an absent-minded poet than a soldier. He had long black hair, wore spectacles, was always untidy and went about so deep in thought that he rarely seemed to know where he was going or why. He was fortunate, or possibly unfortunate, in having a private income. When he left school, being of a very shy and self-conscious nature, he went to work in a large London library and hid himself away from the world behind a pile of books. He lived alone in a flat in Chelsea, where he knew nobody, and for years lived this secluded life, riveting his entire energies on literature and music. For a time he enjoyed life, but then he grew very lonely. Although he craved company, he was too shy to seek it. When the war came he was called up and since then, much to his joy, had been in contact with all types of men.

On this voyage I began to study for my next exams, the First Mate's certificate, for which I could sit after being in charge of a watch for 18 months. It seemed a long way off, but there was a lot that I had to learn.

A raider was reported to be operating in this area, and one morning the Steward woke me early to go to action stations. Just visible was the dim outline of the ship whose movements had aroused the Mate's suspicions. We stood by for a time at the gun, and to our great relief saw the ship slowly disappear into the mist. Soon after, the Old Man gave me instructions to fire three practice rounds of ammunition from the 4.7-inch gun. The gun hadn't been fired for a long time, so we didn't know what condition it was in. The Second Mate and the Carpenter ignited a smoke float and threw it overboard to act as a target. I waited until the range was about 2000 yards and then gave orders to open fire. With the first two shots I straddled the target and the last one fell quite close, which was a pleasing result.

After making slow progress westward we reached the Gulf Stream and the temperature rose into the 70s. My cabin, directly over the boilers, became like an oven. Unless I wanted to stream sweat, I had to remain outside. I discovered that the soldiers were provided with spare hammocks, so I borrowed one. Others whose cabins were also unbearably hot copied the idea and soon were also sleeping out. The first night was a learning experience. Some were foolish enough to sleep up on the poop at the stern, and as the wind was right ahead and there was heavy smoke from the funnel, they awoke next morning black as chimney sweeps, to the vast amusement of those who had been thoughtful enough to sleep forward of the funnel.

We sighted land for the first time in three weeks, and passed a very pleasant morning only a mile or so off the famous pleasure resorts of Palm Beach and Miami. Several motor launches came close, their occupants fishing with apparent deadly earnestness sitting in carefully arranged tiers of easy chairs under awnings and looking neither to left nor to right.

We rounded the reef-tipped southern point of Florida, headed north, and reached Tampa outer bay after a 32-day passage from Scotland. The Pilot came aboard at 6 a.m. as we approached a low coastline covered with palms and intersected by creeks. He told me that his father came to Tampa as a merchant 53 years ago. Tampa was then a small village, and their only communication with the outside world was through local coastal schooners. When one of them arrived, the courthouse bell was rung and all the villagers turned out to help discharge the cargo.

At Tampa, Florida

We arrived at our dock on 9 September. It was about nine miles from the city and getting there entailed a journey of over an hour, walking to a ferry that took us across a narrow stretch of water and then taking a fast, uncomfortable tram. I was upset to find that it was compulsory for blacks to sit at the back and whites at the front. Coming back late at night, we found the ferry not running. We had the options of a long walk round the docks in mosquito-infested areas, or borrowing the ferry and paddling it across using boards as paddles, then returning the ferry towing a punt that we would use for the final crossing back to the ship. We chose the ferry.

The days in port were stifling hot, and after dark, although it grew cooler, we weren't left to enjoy the night as the mosquitoes went into action. These detestable insects were fitted with a silencer that effectively cut out their warning buzz. They quietly approached their objective, then without warning dived to the attack. Even in the face of heavy and determined defences, they continued with great audacity to obtain direct hits and very few of their number were brought down. For the first few days quite a number of us swam off the ship's side. The water was too warm to make it really enjoyable, and also rather dirty. When it was rumoured that, in addition to these drawbacks, there were sharks and barracudas about, enthusiasm for swimming rapidly dwindled.

We visited the Merchant Navy club and the American USO at Tampa and attended some dances, but found the women either could not dance or did so in an entirely different way from us. On every voyage I had a shopping list of things my family and friends would like and could not get at home, so shopping was an important activity. On another visit I went with the Mate and the Second Engineer to Sulphur Springs bathing pools, where the water came from an underground river so the pools were always cool. In addition to the swimming, enjoyable occupations were going down the water chute, being swept round the bend by the current, and swinging on a trapeze suspended over the pool that gave many of the sensations experienced by a trapeze artist without any of the danger.

Our stay was prolonged in order to renew tubes in one of the boilers and make other engine room repairs. Once they were finished we loaded over 6000 tons of phosphate from an elevator that worked at a rate of over a 1000 tons an hour. Our consignment was loaded in one evening! Then we started loading TNT and cordite in the magazines constructed here entirely of wood. All shore leave was stopped and locals working aboard were highly paid. Smoking on deck was prohibited. We felt that the sooner we got rid of the explosives, the better.

Tampa to Sydney, Nova Scotia

We left Tampa on 24 September so deeply laden that at the dock we were sitting on the mud and the tug had its work cut out to pull us clear. We had just started downstream when the Chief Engineer came up to tell us there was engine trouble and a stop was essential. We anchored to allow the repairs to be carried out. Shortly after getting under way again we had to make another stop for further repairs but at last we put to sea. As long as the hot weather lasted I camped out in a hammock, but when we left the Gulf Stream there was a sharp drop in temperature.

The ship became a resting place for all sorts of birds migrating south, and some were quite tame. The Mate approached within a few feet of a large cormorant that was perched on the edge of a lifeboat. It only flapped its wings and hopped away a little, looking at him with mild interest. Later, it laid its head in its wings and snoozed. Another day a hawk came on the scene, and after a short chase caught a small bird, which it took it to the stem to eat, all the time watching for any signs of danger. The little birds were even worse off than we, because war and air raids lasted throughout their lives. At Tampa a little yellow bird joined the ship and lived in the sailors' mess room and the galley, eating flies and cockroaches. It grew so tame that it perched on the sailors' shoulders while they had meals.

The *Beaver* continued to develop problems. Twice we had to stop for engine trouble, and as we approached Sydney a great blast of flame belched out of the funnel, sending everyone running to rig the fire hoses to guard our ammunition magazine. We had difficulty making the landfall approaching Sydney, owing to low visibility caused by mist and rain, but shortly after we had obtained wireless shore bearings the mist lifted and we could see the harbour entrance.

We were at Sydney for a week waiting for the next convoy to leave. The days slipped by uneventfully with little work to do while we lay at anchor. It was a good time to write letters, wash and iron clothes, and mend socks. I got through several books and listened to music on the gramophone. To get some exercise several of us tossed around a heavy medicine ball, and we had several impromptu soccer matches on the after deck between Scottish and English members of the crew, using a stuffed rag as a ball.

I was thinking about my plans for the future. Before the war my idea had been to get my Second Mate's certificate and then go to university for a teaching degree. Now I could not leave the sea until the war ended, and I was loath to throw away my nautical experience and knowledge. I knew that I did not want to spend my life at sea. There were a few shore jobs for seamen such as Board of Trade surveyors, harbour masters and pilots. Each had strict entry requirements and was much sought after. Shipboard life cut me off from so many things I liked to do, such as playing in an orchestra, acting in plays, engaging in sports and helping run a Scout troop. If I got married I would like to know that most of my life would not have to be spent away from my wife and home. I would have to wait until the war ended before there was much I that I could do to further any plans.

Sydney to Glasgow

Our convoy sailed on 11 October, but as we were second to last ship to go out we had an hour or two to wait for our turn. During this period the engineers found yet another thing wrong in the engine room necessitating a delay of several hours. We were all very upset as it meant missing the convoy, spending another week at Sydney, and then a possible change in destination away from our homeport of Glasgow. To our relief the repairs were finished in time for us to catch up with the convoy.

When we were clear of the land we met the full force of a gale. The *Beaver* was encumbered by her heavy cargo and started rolling wildly, pitching and labouring under the big seas that poured across the decks. She gave us such a shaking up that after tea I felt quite seasick and lay down until it was time to go on watch. We secured all the steel doors leading into our accommodation, but even then the alleyways became flooded and most of the cabins were swimming in water. During my evening watch, she took two or three particularly heavy seas on the boat deck that poured down the ventilators into the engineers' cabins and soaked them. A boom of timber used for keeping a lifeboat in place was broken, but otherwise little damage was done. Coming off the night watch, I found water sloshing about in the alleyway and causing a haze by striking the steam heaters. Everything was wet and stuffy and the wild rolling of the ship made a continuous creaking and banging.

On watch the next night it was pitch dark, and because I had been told by the Mate to follow the wrong ship, all the ships seemed to be out of position. When the moon rose I found that we were a long way astern of the convoy; it took the remainder of the watch to catch up. Showers of sparks were issuing from the funnel. I had the hose on the fore deck manned in case any sparks got near the magazines. The *Beaver* gave several repeat performances of this behaviour that made us jumpy as cats because the sparks lit up the ship, acting as a beacon to any submarines or raiders within 20 miles of us. None could have been there, since we had quiet nights. I had nightmares about being on watch and unable to see anything in the pitch dark, and was terrified that I would run into the ship ahead.

After the gale we had a few days of relative calm. I held a night gun drill to give the crew the experience of night conditions. Then we ran into another gale. The *Beaver* was rolling so heavily that it was difficult to remain in my bunk at night and I was constantly waking up to find myself on the point of being thrown onto the floor. Apart from some reading and making up accounts, I spent time off watch sleeping and lying reading on my bunk. The violent rolling and lurching was very tiring and made me feel not seasick but uncomfortable enough to make any activity a great effort.

While we were in the Western Approaches, the Carpenter found a bad leak had started in No. 4 hold. Our pumps were able to cope with the inflow of water so long as the suctions in the hold did not get choked and block the pumps. At last we entered the Firth of Clyde, where the Pilot boarded and took us to an anchorage. To our surprise a large salvage tug and a diver's launch were waiting for us. The message reporting our damage had been wrongly relayed. It had arrived in a form that led our owners to understand that we had been torpedoed and were limping in with an 18-foot hole in our side. The diver plugged up our leak temporarily and we remained at anchor for the night.

Next day we moved to another anchorage where a London firm of stevedores came aboard and discharged the explosives into Dutch coasters. Compared with American stevedores, they handled the explosives in a way that made me nervous. They unloaded big slings of about 30 boxes of TNT at a time, wore hobnailed boots that could cause sparks, and threw the cases around. They got extra pay for the danger, but we got nothing extra. After the explosives were discharged we spent several frustrating days before orders came to proceed up the Clyde to Glasgow. It was nearly a year since I had last been up the river, and I felt the usual thrill of nearing the homeport. When we docked a relieving mate came on board almost at once, so the Second Mate and I were both able to go home.

Voyage 3 – November 1941 to March 1942

Returning from leave, I found the *Beaver* in dry dock where hull plates had to be replaced to stop the leak she had sprung. The repair work was not finished, everything seemed upside down and there were several days' work to be done before the ship would be ready. Everything possible was being done to get the *Beaver* to sea. There were so many superintendents and officials rushing around that they could almost have pushed the ship out. We were in no hurry to go, and the *Beaver* must have known this for she effectively put a stop to sailing by breaking a spindle in the steering gear while it was being tested. Finally on 22 November we went down the river and anchored in the Firth of Clyde where convoys gathered.

We were exceedingly lucky in missing the previous convoy, as they encountered such bad weather that they could make no headway and were so battered that they had to return to the Clyde for fresh bunkers and some for repairs. While at anchor, we had a few days' breathing space in which to tidy up and straighten out the confusion and mess left by the Glasgow carpenters who had installed the lockers now required in the lifeboats. In place of the old-fashioned biscuits, tinned milk and meat kept in each lifeboat, new regulations required there to be specially prepared biscuits, pemmican, chocolate and malted milk tablets. I divided these up and stowed them in the new lockers.

Glasgow to Philadelphia

On 28 November our convoy slipped out under cover of darkness. Once clear of the land we ran into a heavy swell left over from the last gale, and shortly after the wind picked up from the south-east until a fresh gale was blowing. Many of the ships in the convoy, including the *Beaver*, were going out in ballast, which meant that a large portion of their hull was exposed to the force of the wind, making the ships very difficult to handle. When the turning power of the rudder was overcome by the power of the wind, the ship became uncontrollable. The convoy became a straggled bunch of ships trailing after the Commodore. The *Beaver* was jumping about like a frightened horse, pitching and rolling violently, vibrating as the propeller came out of water and thrashing the air, and shuddering as the bows crashed down into a trough. All the cabins were in shambles and anything not secured was flung about. During watches below I spent most of the time lying on my bunk reading or trying to sleep. The latter was very difficult as an extra heavy roll would be enough to almost throw me out on the deck. After the first night, I tilted the mattress so that it sloped down towards the bulkhead, put a line of cushions along the bulkhead and slept in the trough so formed. The temperature had not yet been below freezing point, but when the wind became more northerly it was bitterly cold. During the frequent violent squalls of rain, hail and sleet, it was a thankless task keeping a lookout, as the elements cut my face and almost blinded me.

Our crew was older and less cheerful than on the last voyage. Captain Blacklock had taken over from Captain Johnson. He must have been between 50 and 60 years old, and was short in stature and inconspicuous in appearance. He was retired when the war started, and was running a farm with his brother-in-law in Perthshire. He was asked to return to sea; three weeks before joining this ship he had been ploughing with a tractor on their farm. He used the old sea form of address of "Mister Mate" when speaking to me. He had been at sea most of his life, and his world appeared to extend little further than the decks of his ships. Our previous Captain Johnson was exceedingly efficient, very particular about details and had the main say in everything that went on in every department. He was a very good master for me to sail with, as he kept an eye on all my work, taught me a great deal and demanded a high state of efficiency in everything I did. Captain Blacklock was probably just as efficient, but instead of having his finger in every pie, he left every department to run its own way, did not interfere with any methods and systems that might have been adopted by different individuals, and apart from visits to the bridge when we were at sea, he stayed behind the scenes and did not want to be bothered with details. Provided you knew your work, this Master was easier to work with and left you more to rely on your own judgement.

On 8 December the news came through that the Japanese had bombed Pearl Harbor and declared war on the United States. They also invaded British territory in the Far East, and Britain declared war on Japan. The United States had not yet made a formal declaration, but it was expected at any time. It was now a world war with a vengeance, but on the *Beaver* our lives went on as usual.

With the calmer weather, I was able to do more. I developed a good laundry apparatus. The Cook lent me a big wooden keg that had held salt pork, which I used as a washtub. I found a rubbing board that had been on the ship for a long time, and obtained hot water from a big tank over the fire in the galley. With this I was able to wash 18 pieces of clothing. I also spent spare time studying and reading Hitler's *Mein Kampf*. His observations on the psychology of the masses, propaganda and leadership showed clearly the methods he was using.

The new Mate had very poor eyesight; at night, unless there was a moon, he often lost the ship ahead. When I relieved him at the end of his watch, I had trouble in getting back to our correct position. One night we completely lost the convoy. I spent an anxious two hours peering through binoculars before sighting it. When off the bridge I kept out of the Mate's way. He was terribly bitter, cynical and sarcastic, and had not the intelligence to express himself in an interesting way. He was a good practical sailor, but of very little use as an officer. He must have had a terribly disappointing and unhappy life to make him into the person he had become.

The Senior Wireless Operator kept daylight watches with us on the bridge to assist with the signalling. He was about 40 years of age, small and wiry, with long straight hair that obstinately stuck straight up after withstanding years of brushing back. My first impression of him was unfavourable, as he shook hands with great heartiness, slapped me on the back and addressed me with great enthusiasm, saying "Hello, old man, terribly glad to meet you", at which onslaught my coldness increased in proportion to his familiarity. I learned he was a London taxi driver, and had worked as a technician for the BBC. He related an incident when he was a taxi driver as if it was so trifling that the effect was funny. He had "picked up a lady fare", who had instructed him to drive to a hotel. On arrival he carried her cases up to her room. Having performed the task and while he was still in her room, she shut the door and told him that unless he gave her all the money he had she would scream the house down. Knowing that if she did so he would probably have his cab driver's licence taken from him, he knocked her out with a punch on the jaw, removed his fare from her handbag and quietly departed.

One night during my evening watch it was very dark, and owing to the bad weather the convoy was well spread out. A glow suddenly appeared in the sky astern, like a loom of some flames below the horizon. The light grew in intensity, and then after flaring up so as to light the eastern sky it dwindled away and disappeared. It must have been a ship on fire, whether through enemy action or not we could only surmise. Any other time we would have turned back to see if we could be of any assistance, but now we must not. It might have been an enemy ruse to lure a ship away from the convoy, or a ship really on fire with a submarine standing by to sink any rescue ship. As our responsibility for our crew and ship came first, we had to go on, fervently hoping that one of the small fast escorts, less liable to being caught in a trap, would go back.

The Old Man was always nervous with ships around us in convoy, and after we lost the convoy on several occasion he decided that we would set off on our own.

The question uppermost in everyone's mind was whether we were going to reach Philadelphia for Christmas. We had eight days to get there. The weather tantalized us by providing a calm sea and every sign of good weather, and then a few hours later dashed our hopes with a gale. We were beginning to feel really optimistic when the *Beaver* decided it was high time she had a rest, so she blew a boiler tube and developed troubles in her condenser. We stopped shortly after 3 p.m., and although we started up again by 7.30 p.m., she moved slowly. Twice more we had to slow down for leaking boiler tubes. We ran into some bitterly cold weather with snow. Ice formed on the rigging, and we had to put steam on the winches to prevent them from freezing up.

At Philadelphia

On 23 December we reached the mouth of the Delaware River, after a passage of 27 days. With a favourable tide and by pushing the *Beaver* to her full speed, we hoped to reach Philadelphia by evening. We were out of luck because we ran into a fog and had to anchor overnight. We docked next day at noon. The agents and immigration authorities kindly rushed through the numerous formalities necessary to get us shore passes. Money was sent aboard for the Old Man so that the crew could draw on their wages, and with everyone lending a hand the crew was free to go ashore by 6 p.m. on Christmas Eve.

On Christmas Day I was on duty aboard. By lunchtime I was feeling pretty miserable and rather homesick, so I asked Sparks if he was willing to help me serve the stewards while they had Christmas dinner. He willingly agreed, so after we had eaten an excellent dinner we took charge of the pantry, borrowed the stewards' jackets and rang the bell for them to sit down. We roped in the Second Engineer and Third Engineer to help and had great fun dishing up the turkey and plum pudding, with Sparks waiting with great efficiency in the saloon. The Second Engineer, acting as pantry man, got into serious trouble at the end of the meal by going into the saloon and sitting down with his feet on the table. Fortunately the Mate went ashore before dinner. That morning he had been semi-drunk and had wasted most of my morning following me around talking, running people down, grumbling and using filthy language. By the time we had washed up I was feeling far happier, and spent a quiet afternoon and evening reading *A Farewell to Arms* and listening to a broadcast of Dickens's *Christmas Carol*.

This voyage we were loading steel, cases of tinned meat, salmon, milk and other foodstuffs. It gave me far more satisfaction to take home a cargo of this nature than scrap iron or phosphate. I was busy most of the day seeing that the bilges had been cleaned out properly, and in the evening started a plan to show where the different kinds of cargo were being loaded in the holds. I turned in early. Shortly after midnight I was awakened by the noise of a violent argument going on between the Mate, who was very drunk, and Boyall, the night watchman. The Mate was accusing Boyall of not doing his duty and being away from the gangway and Boyall was replying that he was entitled to go for his supper. Then Boyall came in and asked me, as officer on duty, whether he had the right to have supper during the night. He had, so I took his side. The Mate became more abusive, calling Boyall insulting names. Suddenly he struck Boyall, and it looked like the start of a fight. I jumped out of my bunk and went between them. Luckily at that moment the Cook appeared on the scene and forcibly restrained the Mate while I quieted Boyall, who was trembling with rage. The Cook got the Mate into the pantry, and after telling Boyall to keep out of the Mate's way, we got the Mate into his cabin after a lot of trouble. I had just got to sleep again when the gangway guard woke me up to settle a dispute between one of the army gunners, who was drunk, and a taxi driver. The gunner had no money to pay for his taxi, so had come aboard and hidden. I told the night watchman to find him and eventually got the matter squared away.

On New Year's Eve I expected trouble from the Mate when he came back aboard, so I slept from eight in the evening and was called just before midnight. As the New Year came in we struck 16 bells, eight for the old year and eight for the new, which is an old sea tradition. Then I followed the Scottish custom of first footing (visiting) those on board. Soon after, the Mate staggered aboard, a paper bag full of tins of beer in one hand and a battered trilby perched on his head. I wished him a happy New Year, and then by flattery, persuasion and sympathetic listening kept him quiet. I left him and sent in Boyall with instructions to do the same and to condole with the Mate's distress of mind. Boyall did the task with great diplomacy and had a drink with the Mate. When I thought the time was ripe, I went in and, in a theatrical manner, bawled out Boyall for not attending to his job and ticked off the Mate for keeping a man from his duty. The performance went through without a hitch, and we got the Mate to turn in without a fight. Next morning breakfast was badly delayed, as all the cooks and stewards except the Chief Steward were absent on "French leave". The Mate was still drunk, so I kept out of his way. That evening was quiet except for a mattress going on fire because of a careless smoker.

During the remainder of our stay at Philadelphia, we continued to have trouble with the Mate and the crew. On returning from a shore visit, the gangway guard told me that the Mate had come aboard drunk and attacked Wee Jimmy, the Second Mate. He had defended himself with a heavy torch so that the Mate had the worst of the encounter. The sailors gave a good deal of trouble by going "adrift" for days on end, getting drunk and doing very little work. Most of the trouble was due to the Mate misbehaving and letting the crew get away with their absences from the ship. He was afraid that if he used his authority they could retaliate by refusing to sail with a mate who had poor vision. Some allowance for the crew's behaviour was appropriate, since it was a festive season, but after shutting my eyes to a few faults and giving a man one chance, I would have had no hesitation in logging and fining every subsequent offence.

The *Beaver* had new tubing fitted in two of her boilers, a job which had been waiting to be done since last July when the Lloyd's surveyor condemned all the boilers. Much other work was also been done in the engine room. Since the two patches that were put on the bow at Glasgow had not stopped the leaks, they were reinforced with cement boxes.

We received wonderful hospitality while in Philadelphia. As soon as we docked, a representative of the Merchant Navy Club came aboard to determine what sort of entertainments we liked. When we went to the club we were given invitations to visit people's homes and free tickets to concerts, theatres and dances. They gave us a pass to the Pennsylvania Athletic Club, where the Second Wireless Operator and I enjoyed the luxury of a splendid swimming pool. The Second Mate, Wee Jimmy and I took it in turn to either be on duty on the ship or be free to spend time ashore. An English family who had been evacuated from England invited me for the day to their home in the country. After dinner we went for a walk in the woods, inspected the children's tree house and played some games. After spending so long at sea, it was a great treat to spend time with a congenial family in a lovely setting. I achieved one of my ambitions by attending a concert of the Philadelphia Symphony Orchestra conducted by Eugene Ormandy. At the end he wished everyone the season's greetings, and as an encore conducted Sousa's great march "The Stars and Stripes Forever". It brought the audience to their feet cheering and applauding.

The family I had spent the day with invited me to go with them to New York to see *Aida* at the Metropolitan Opera. The drive to New York was exciting, and I was spellbound by the music and the spectacle. I arranged a 36-hour visit with the McCulloughs in New York. They were the same age as my grandparents, whom they had first met when on holiday in Switzerland. Whenever friends of the McCulloughs went to England my grandparents entertained them, and vice versa. The dinner the first evening I arrived, besides being a meal, was a ceremony performed by candlelight with beautifully decorated trencher tools and an efficient gliding maid who served the delicious dishes with a kind of reverence towards them. The meal was accompanied by easy flowing conversation. My hosts then took me to see a performance of *Macbeth*. The room I slept in had a private bathroom, so I had the luxury of a hot bath before going to bed. Next day we lunched at the Waldorf Astoria Hotel, where after walking over thick carpets and being addressed by obsequious attendants we ate amidst a great display of luxury. I was in uniform, but felt eclipsed by the gorgeous trappings of the hotel porters. That evening Mrs McCullough arranged for me to go to the Metropolitan Opera with a girl to see *The Marriage of Figaro* with Ezio Pinza singing. After the opera I returned to my hosts' home, said goodbye and took a night train back to Philadelphia. It had been a wonderful experience and I had especially enjoyed the warmth and kindness of the McCulloughs. The visit was like a dream of luxury, but I was not sorry to wake up.

Philadelphia to New York

On 11 January we loaded explosives. When we tried to leave, the *Beaver* couldn't cant round to head downstream as the tide was bringing down great quantities of ice that piled up against her side. We had to give up the attempt to cant, and anchored until the change in tide swung the ship so that she headed downstream. During the night the Pilot took us down the Delaware. By noon we had left the river and were at sea bound for Halifax.

After lunch I was tidying up the confusion in my cabin that invariably followed a busy stay in port, when Wee Jimmy burst into my cabin to tell me we that had received a wireless message, not in code, telling all British ships within a 300-mile radius of Nantucket to proceed immediately to the nearest port. No reason was given for the order and we guessed it was because German submarines were beginning to attack ships on the east coast of the United States. I went to tell the gunners to have everything ready in case we were attacked. A little later the Old Man told them all to stand by their guns. Our course was altered and we headed for New York. We showed no lights during the hours of darkness and had to keep an extra good look out, as there was no moon and there was a considerable amount of coastal traffic. Later in the evening reports came in of ships being sunk near by. The job of the submarines was made easier because the unrestricted bright lights on shore silhouetted ships.

Next morning we picked up the New York pilot who took us to the explosives anchorage. No one came to give us instructions. The following morning the Old Man went ashore for instructions and to obtain new water breakers (containers) for the lifeboats, as ours had been broken by the water in them freezing. He returned just before tea with two pilots and ordered the whole ship's company to muster in the saloon. In a state of great curiosity, everyone hurriedly gathered. The Old Man told us that it would be impossible to obtain the new water breakers before tomorrow. The government wanted us to sail immediately. We were to go to Halifax, hugging the coast all the way. A coastal pilot was on board ready to take the ship round. Were we willing to take a chance and go without the breakers, or would we rather stay, as we were entitled to do, until the breakers arrived? A short silence followed; everyone waited for someone else to speak first. Then the Second Mate and I said we would go, and then the whole crew agreed.

New York to Halifax

We got under way as soon as the engineers were ready and steamed out into the light haze that was hanging over the mouth of the Hudson. Our route took us through the Cape Cod Canal. En route we received news that two merchant ships had been torpedoed. One was 60 miles out to sea and the other at a point that we had passed a few hours earlier. An icy cutting wind was blowing from the north-west and the spray froze as it landed on deck. While on watch there was nothing out of the ordinary to occupy my mind except seeing that the steam pipes, winch cylinders and whistle did not freeze up. A thick mantle of ice gathered on the fore deck and made the *Beaver* appear far more beautiful in her glistening white than in her dull coat of grey. Even the rails and rigging were delicately laced in ice. When we reached Halifax on 17 January we were unusually glad to enter port, as six ships hade been lost owing to enemy action since we had left New York. The Pilot having brought us up the channel, we passed through a long narrow neck on which the town of Halifax lies, and entered a sheltered basin that was large enough for over a hundred ships to anchor.

At Halifax

Our stay became far longer than we had anticipated because more boiler trouble delayed us and made us miss the convoy we were to have sailed with. There being little tide and quiet weather, we had no worries over the anchor dragging, so apart from being up and dressed during anchor watches, we were free to get any needed work done. It gave me ample time to get all the lifesaving gear examined, attend to the flags needing repair, and correct the code books. It was a very leisurely existence as we just worked when we liked. I generally spent the morning for the ship and the rest of the day for myself. I was able to get a great pile of laundry done, much written in my diary, and all sorts of odd jobs finished such as mending, tidying up, reading and studying for the mate's exams. The Mate gave me some canvas to make a sea bag on which I sewed for an hour or two a day. There was about 40 feet of seam to be sewn before the bag was finished.

One morning I woke up to find a blizzard blowing and visibility reduced to one or two ship lengths. We were to have gone out in convoy that morning, but since any movement of ships would have been crazy, the orders were to postpone. During the afternoon a ship dragged her anchors and crashed into another ship. It was 16 degrees Fahrenheit and perishing cold outside. Even so, the stewards challenged Jimmy, the Wireless Operator and me to a snowball fight, and that night we had a battle up on the boat deck.

We finally got under way in convoy. A gale was blowing on our port beam, and even with the helm hard a-starboard the *Beaver* would not answer to it. As a result we were unable to keep our position in the convoy. We made a thorough examination of the steering gear, but no defects were apparent. During the evening an alteration of course made it possible to get back close to the convoy, but the steering was still bad and it would have been dangerous to return to our station.

With the bitter cold, heavy ice began forming on the fore deck from the spray and seas coming aboard. Next morning the fore deck was almost unrecognizable. From the bridge down the superstructure and decks were sheathed in ice. It was as though some giant had wrapped cotton wool over the ship. The space under the forecastle head had assumed the appearance of a fairy grotto glistening and sparkling in the sunshine.

After breakfast we made another examination of the steering gear. The younger engineers climbed down a ladder from the stern to look at the rudder, a heroic task with an icy cold wind and the ship pitching. Some reported that the rudder was not turning as much as it should. Others were of the opinion that the rudder went hard over but slowly came back amidships even when the helm was kept hard over. The Old Man was terribly worried, wondering whether to carry on and probably lose the convoy as soon as a westerly wind sprang up, or return to Halifax unescorted through an area where there had recently been much enemy submarine activity. Then, if nothing was found to be wrong with the rudder, he would be in an awkward position because officials would wonder why he returned at great expense and loss of time to the ship. I did not envy his having to make the decision. At 10 o'clock we signalled the escort "Returning to Halifax owing to rudder trouble".

Later in the day the wind dropped and steering became easier. While having tea I heard the Old Man shouting that he wanted someone to signal by Morse since neither he nor the Mate were any use at it. When I shot up to the bridge, I was told a light had been flashing right ahead, but had stopped before I got to the bridge. At the same time a wireless message came through reporting an enemy submarine a few miles distant of us. We instantly manned the guns and phoned down to the engine room for all the speed the *Beaver* was capable of. The light off Halifax was visible, and for the next hour black smoke belched from the funnel and the *Beaver* was trembling in every plate as she stormed along at just over nine knots. Everyone was keeping a lookout, scanning the moonlit sea. We reached the Pilot, who took us up to the explosives anchorage where we anchored for the night.

Sixteen tense days followed while we remained at anchor trying to solve the mystery of why the *Beaver* had refused to steer. Several investigations were made of the rudder and steering gear; all concluded that it was not defective. Finally a diver went down and found that a 30-foot section of the port bilge keel was flapping loose. The purpose of the bilge keels, which ran along the outsides of the ship on the curve between the sides and bottom, was to dampen the rolling movement. It was unlikely that this was the source of the steering problem. Another possible source of the steering problem was the trim of the ship. She was more down in the bow than the stern because of the way that the cargo had been loaded, and the weight of the ice on the fore deck might have accentuated this when we were at sea. To change the trim we started discharging cargo from the forward hold and loading it in the aft hold. A few hours later, the shore authorities decided that the job would take several days; they wanted us to sail in convoy the next day. An angry shore superintendent ordered the cargo put back where it had been. There was a nasty atmosphere among the seniors shore officials, who were looking for a scapegoat to account for the ship's delay. The Shore Superintendent accused our Captain and us mates of being afraid of going to sea.

The Empire Beaver (*Reproduced with kind permission
from the National Maritime Museum, Greenwich, London*)

Second Mate ('wee Jimmy'), Radio Operator and author

*Convoy gathering in Bedford Basin, Halifax Harbour (Reproduced with
kind permission from the Maritime Command Museum and Department
of National Defence, Canada)*

On the day the next convoy was to have sailed, the Captain summoned the Mate, the Second Mate and me to his cabin. He showed us the surveyor's report on the port bilge and said he was unwilling to sail without the trim of the ship being changed. He also felt that the damaged bilge keel would cause a leak. The question was whether the ship was in fit condition to cross the Atlantic in convoy. The prevailing wind would be westerly across the Atlantic, and this meant we would have following winds – the conditions under which the *Beaver* had refused to steer. This made our chances of being able to remain with the convoy slight. The delay involved great expense and might cause the apples in our cargo to go bad, but that was a smaller expense than sending the *Beaver* out with a good chance she would be lost at sea. Our first consideration should be for the ship, not ourselves. The Captain told us he had decided to refuse to sail and wanted our agreement, which we gave. He went ashore and when he returned the shifting of the cargo started.

Next day a representative of the Ministry of Shipping came aboard to make an enquiry. The other mates and I were called on to verify the facts of what had happened and the officials had a long session with the Old Man. After the shifting of cargo was completed, the *Beaver* was two feet down at the stern. While this was going on we had found a separate problem. The ice had carried away one of the air pipes to an oil tank and seawater had got into the oil. A barge came alongside and pumped out the contaminated oil, and replaced it with fresh oil. We were all fed up with the hanging around. I had reached a state where I had become so restless, depressed, and bored that I felt like doing something crazy. I had no one here with whom I could really talk and exchange ideas, and I often missed Kennedy, who had been such a good companion on the *Elysia*. I could stand a great deal of my own company, but sometimes I had so much of it that I became lonely and stagnant.

It helped to pass the time to listen to the wireless. On 15 February Churchill spoke and tea was delayed so that we could all listen. Strong criticism was arising at home against the government because the Japanese had recently invaded the Malay Peninsula and were driving south towards their objective of Singapore, generally believed to be impregnable. A squadron of German battleships had slipped through the English Channel when favoured by low visibility, without any losses. It was in the face of this criticism that he spoke. His oratory was as brilliant as ever, but he gave away very little information.

To give the crew a break, the Captain allowed half of us to go ashore one day and the other half the next day. I went ashore to find the town swamped with servicemen wandering around looking for entertainment. There was little to do except go to the pictures and dances where there were so many men to every girl it was hardly worth going. I went to two films, with a gap for eating in between. It was depressing, and I returned to the ship with a headache.

Halifax to Liverpool

At last we were on the move again, after a stay of 29 days. We steamed down the harbour in the long line of ships that would make up the convoy. With the change in the trim of the ship we had no further problem steering. During the passage to Liverpool we had the kind of winter weather that we had come to expect on the North Atlantic: a succession of gales, alternating with brief periods of good weather.

On the second day out from Halifax the sea was still smooth and the slab ice had become heavier, spread in large fields with broad stretches of open water between them. The log that rotated in the water (to measure distance the ship travelled) started skidding along the ice instead of turning in the water, so as it had become useless we took it in. At night the stars were reflected in the ice and looked like little fairy lights skimming along beside the ship. Shortly before noon the wind began rising; we were grateful to leave the ice astern.

On 24 February the Carpenter's sounding of the bilges showed a suspicious rise of water in No. 4 port bilge, indicating that we might have sprung a leak. The pumps were started and were able to cope with the water, but after the Carpenter continued to sound the bilges, it became apparent that *Beaver* had another leak. The Bosun found there was also water in the forepeak. As the leaks got worse, the bilge pumps had to work almost continuously. Clearly the *Beaver* had found another reason to extend our time in the next port, and I only hoped that she had not slipped up in her judgement and sprung a leak too serious for us to reach port.

On the evening of 3 March there was a full moon, and the sea had settled down to a slight swell. Later during the watch it began to grow darker and the moon began to diminish in size. It was not until it had become a crescent that I realized this must be an eclipse and went down to ask the Old Man, who verified the fact from the Nautical Almanac. He came up to see it. Through the telescope the shadow of the penumbra could be seen crossing the moon, the moon becoming fainter until it disappeared. The slowly gathering darkness was quite eerie, and without a rational explanation of the phenomenon I think I would have been very frightened. The Captain said that a gale often follows an eclipse, and it did blow hard the next day.

On 5 March we sighted the British coast and the homeward gallop started. The convoy Commodore left the stragglers behind. Then we ran into a heavy snowstorm that made it difficult to see the ship ahead of us in the convoy. Navigating around the British coast had become increasingly difficult as almost all the lighthouses and radio direction-finding stations had stopped operating to make navigation for the Germans more difficult. The Commodore ordered the convoy to heave to until the weather improved. Shortly after midnight it cleared. When an enemy aircraft warning came through, we had to decide which incurred the lesser risk: leaving on the navigation lights with the risk of being sighted by enemy aircraft, or proceeding without lights and chancing collision with other ships. We chose the latter, and although the night was pitch dark we made landfall before dawn. Later the convoy broke up, and we proceeded to Holyhead, in Wales, where the explosives were unloaded. Two days later we moved on to Liverpool to discharge our main cargo.

This was our last voyage on the *Beaver*, because news came aboard that the old girl had been sold to the Norwegians and we would all be leaving. I had had a very happy year aboard her, visiting interesting ports, gaining experience of ships and human nature, and having my first real taste of responsibility. I was sorry to leave. The Captain said that he would do everything he could to have Jimmy and me with him on the next ship he was given. I hoped we would sail with him again as we understood each other and worked well together.

After we left the *Beaver* she was renamed *Mohauk* by the Norwegians. We later learned that in December 1943, nine months after we left her, she was sunk by a mine in the Thames Estuary.

CHAPTER 4

Tahsinia

Time ashore in Britain – March to May 1942

When I left the *Empire Beaver* there was no definite word of any vacant berths on Runciman's ships (the Anchor Line was part of Runciman). I went to see the Marine Superintendent in Glasgow, who offered me a berth as Third Mate on a new cargo ship, the *Tahsinia*, that was being built at Sunderland on the east coast of England, and was to make a voyage to India. It would be a month or so before she would be ready, and in the meantime he wished me to stand by the Anchor Line ship *California* that was being converted from an armed merchant cruiser to a troop ship at Southampton. If I accepted the offer I would be made a permanent employee of the company and kept on after getting my Mate's and Master Mariner's certificates. Another attraction was a trip to the south coast of England with all expenses paid and later a stay on the east coast while the new ship was being completed. This was a good offer and would enable me to spend time with my family and friends, so I accepted.

After two weeks on leave I was instructed to travel south to Southampton. I had only a few hours in which to return home from the Anchor Line office in Glasgow, pack, return to Glasgow, and catch the night train to London. I got to the train with 15 minutes to spare. Several of the senior officials of the Anchor Line were also on the train. On the following two days at a hotel before moving aboard the *California*, I had the twofold benefits of pleasant conversation with the officials and their having the chance to get to know me.

The four weeks that followed was almost like a holiday, as there was little work to do, we lived in comfort and I was able to go ashore nearly every evening and at weekends. The air raid sirens, which I had almost forgotten, sounded several times a day, but rarely did anything serious happen. For two or three nights we had heavy gunfire and bombs dropped within a few miles, but nothing came close to the ship. Generally the raiders passed overhead to objectives further north. Southampton had been transformed by the air raids, not only physically but socially. The streets of the town were lined with great piles of rubble and dusty skeletons of what had been shops, houses and churches. Having death always near their door made people realize how good life was, and for the time being had swept away many social taboos and conventions. Few persons were to be seen during the day, but twice a week they came flocking in for the dances held in the great guildhall of the new Civic Centre. The dancers were mainly from the services, various ranks being represented, from privates and ordinary seaman to captains and majors, not in the slightest embarrassed by one another's presence and mixing freely. There was an easy, happy-go-lucky, atmosphere in which it was easy to make friends even for those who were shy. I was delighted to find so many tall girls who were good dancers. One girl I danced with was six feet tall. Being able to take large strides, we moved among the other couples like a destroyer going through a convoy.

My grandmother and an aunt lived nearby on the Isle of Wight. Over the weekends I would get a steamer from Southampton to Cowes and then cycle on a borrowed bike to their home at Seaview. I had spent holidays with them as a child and was very fond of them. They gave me a great welcome.

On 4 May I signed off the *California* and returned home on the overnight train. Before joining the *Tahsinia* I went round seeing various friends and saying goodbye. It seemed a major going-away compared with the voyages to America, for the duration of the voyage would be long and uncertain and little mail would get to us from home.

Tahsinia – *May 1942 to March 1943*

On 8 May I travelled south to Sunderland by train and went straight to Doxford's Yard, where the *Tahsinia* had been built. Since the ship had not yet been handed over from the builder to the Anchor Line, I was directed to an office that had been put at our disposal. There I met J. McCormack, the First Mate, and L.H. Smith, the Second Mate. Until the following Monday we lived ashore, going down to the ship during the day to check gear and stores and to get acquainted with her layout. I was eager to move into my new home, found hotel life unsettling, and was glad when the ship was handed over from the shipbuilder to our company so that we could move into our cabins, unpack our gear and settle down. My cabin was rather small, but comfortably furnished and with plenty of places to stow my gear.

A few days later we pulled away from Doxford's Yard and, helped by tugs, went down to the deep-water wharf where we lay overnight taking on fuel and water. There was a vast amount of work for us to do, such as checking and sorting out equipment and stowing it where it belonged, making lists of what was missing, and becoming familiar with the ship. It was work that would have to be done sooner or later, so the sooner everything was shipshape the better. We dry docked to have the bottom painted. On the following day we went round to Newcastle on the river Tyne, and on the way had our gun trials, with some weapons I had not seen before.

Because we were in Newcastle for almost three weeks loading cargo, I had plenty of opportunities to visit relatives, using for travel a second-hand bike I bought in Sunderland. Mother stopped for two nights to visit the ship. After tea, where Mother met nearly all the officers, I showed her round the ship. Before she left I introduced her to the Captain and his wife. Mother really seemed to enjoy her visit, and I was glad that she had a picture of my home and the people with whom I would live. The Mate had just got married, so the Second Mate and I worked extra hours to enable him to get as much free time as possible with his wife. While in port the ship's company did not see much of one another, but I was impressed by their willing and unselfish cooperation, which forecast a happy ship.

Newcastle to Durban, South Africa

We sailed from the Tyne to Methil Roads in the Firth of Forth, where we had a day in much appreciated idleness. It was almost the first time since joining the *Tahsinia* that I felt that we had the work in hand. Everything had been sorted out, arranged, checked and put in place. On 21 June we sailed in convoy for the trip round the north of Scotland. It was uneventful, although the signal was hoisted that air attack was expected. We were not disappointed at their non-appearance. Along the north coast there was a moderate swell, making us realize that the *Tahsinia* was going to be very uncomfortable in bad weather. The way our cargo was stowed made her very stiff, and gave her a quick jerky roll.

This voyage we had two apprentices, and I sympathized with their seasickness as my memories of seasickness were vivid. Coming down the west coast, we parted company with the convoy in order to have a speed trial. We steamed off ahead, with the diesel engine's chugging "I think I can, I think I can" as the engines rotated. Compared with a steam ship the diesel engine was terribly noisy, but after a time we became hardly conscious of the sound. We anchored in Loch Linnhe near Oban, a most beautiful spot. The Second Mate had been experiencing severe headaches and the day we anchored he was feeling ill and had a rash. He went ashore to see the doctor, who said he had German measles, and word came that we were to pack his gear and have it ready to send ashore. Everyone was sorry that he was not coming with us, for he was very popular. We were sailing the same night and arrangements were made to get an Anchor Line officer who was on leave at his home in Ardrishaig. A car was sent for him, and he reached the ship as a replacement for the Second Mate an hour before we sailed in convoy on 24 June.

After rounding the north coast of Ireland, we headed south. For several days we experienced dense fog, often accompanied by rain. The ships managed to stick together by the aid of sound signals, luck and fog buoys. The buoys were towed astern of every ship on a thin wire 600 feet long, and threw up a spout of water. In theory one manoeuvred one's ship until the fog buoy of the ship ahead was just beside the bridge and then tried to remain in the same position relative to the buoy. In practice, it was almost impossible to do so, but if one were directly astern of a ship, and coming up on her, the fog buoy was a valuable indication that one was getting close.

While in convoy submarines were reported to be close, and one of our escort vessels picked up a boatload of survivors from a torpedoed ship. They said another lifeboat was adrift, and the following night it was sighted. A ship with spare accommodations dropped out of the convoy to pick up the survivors. For a week we were visible at night because there was unwelcome bright moonlight. We were passing uncomfortably close to Dakar on the African coast, where submarines had been active. Several ships, including ours, were ordered to proceed independently.

I was able to keep busy in my spare time playing chess, studying and boxing. The junior wireless operator, Carter (nicknamed Ivan because he has a long woolly beard), enjoyed playing chess. We were about equal in skill, and had long and strenuous tussles. We had been assigned the same lifeboat. In case we were torpedoed, I packed a chess set so that we could play while adrift. I spent part of every afternoon studying for the Mate's certificate. In order to study more effectively I made a weekly time sheet showing the amount of time I should spend on each of the exam subjects, and I tried to adhere to the schedule. Sometimes I was interrupted by the Mate coming in for a yarn, and this created a dilemma: should I be social at the cost of losing study time, or should I get work done at the cost of being unsociable and possibly offending the Mate? I decided that, on this long voyage, it was more important to remain on good terms with everyone.

I enjoyed boxing with a set of gloves one of the crew brought aboard. My best sparring partner was one of the army sergeants on board who was over six foot, weighed 13 stone and was in good shape. He knew nothing much about boxing (thank goodness), and apart from his superiority in weight we were well matched. The first day we were shy of each other, but on the following days the boxing became hard and fast and resulted in minor facial damage such as split lips. We then decided to take a few days off. We found some rope and skipped on top of one of the big crates stowed on deck that contained a fighter plane.

On 29 June we entered the tropics; it became increasingly hot. The Old Man laid down no rules about dress, so most of the crew closely approached nudism in their clothes or lack of them. When off the bridge I wore a pair of gym shorts and sandals, then added a shirt when on watch. We crossed the equator but held no ceremony because the decks had recently been oiled and were still sticky.

This voyage was my first experience of having an apprentice (Morrison) on watch with me. When I first went to sea I had difficulty discovering what actions were considered right and wrong, and had to find out by the painful method of trial and error. To prevent such a situation with Morrison, I gave him an outline of his duties and told him that if he did his work efficiently and gave his mind to what he was doing, I would help him with his studies and training. He kept his side of the bargain with only a few lapses, so I kept mine. He proved useful running messages and making supper for me, and I encouraged him to study and questioned him on what he had read. He was thoroughly likable, eager to learn and obliging, and we got on well.

I had been reading *An Outline of Abnormal Psychology*, in which a chapter dealt with the interpretation of dreams. One of my recurring dreams was that I was killed, and unable to hear all the nice (wishful thinking) things that people would say about me. Why this dream? Maybe it was because at sea I was starved of admiration and affection and away from friends who I felt liked and in some ways admired me. Not wishing to appear selfish and vain, I strongly repressed these desires and they only escaped in my dreams. As far as I could remember I did not have such dreams when I was at home. I believe one of the reasons that seamen so often think about women, and when ashore seek their company, is that women, being sympathetic, affectionate and good restorers of self-confidence, make up for the starvation of those things at sea.

As we continued south, the weather grew colder and the nights closed in earlier. For the first few weeks of this passage I enjoyed the quiet of the watches, as I had an ample supply of thoughts and memories from my time in Britain to keep my mind occupied. Then as my stock of things to think about dwindled, I daydreamed more. As this was not conducive to my contentment and general happiness, I tried to harness my imagination to some definite object such as writing a play or story, or doing work for the ship. When on watch and too tired to guide my thoughts, and if no one else was on the bridge, I would recite poetry or sing.

We reached Durban and anchored in the bay. Four days later the Pilot came aboard and took us alongside the oil wharf. When the agent came aboard, he told us that the *Elysia*, on which I had been an apprentice for over three years, had been sunk in the Mozambique Channel. Two Japanese surface raiders had attacked her on 5 June 1942 and riddled her with shells, but the gallant Old Lady would not go under so they finished her off with a torpedo. Even then she remained on the surface, her bow pointing to the skies for a few minutes, before she went to her final resting place. The starboard boats were shot to pieces, but most of the crew got away on the port boats and life rafts. The survivors were picked up some hours later by a hospital ship; one boat was missing, which contained a stewardess, the Chief Steward, the Third Mate, and 16 Indian Ratings. Many of my friends had been aboard her. I tried, without success, to get news of the names of the survivors. My affection for the *Elysia* and those I knew on her was very great, and the news came as a shock.

We were not allowed to go ashore in Durban. Everyone was disappointed as we had been aboard for five weeks. The Captain told us that we had been ordered to go to Suez instead of Bombay. After the recent thrust of Rommel in Egypt to near Cairo, we had guessed we might be diverted and so the news did not come as a surprise. If things got worse we might have to evacuate British troops. On receiving this news much wit was expended on the subject of enemy subs, aircraft and raiders. The ready laughter it evoked showed how fully everyone realized the trip might be a nasty one. My brother Olaf was with the Eighth Army in Egypt and I hoped to be able to contact him.

Durban to Suez

I had always wanted to try my hand at hair cutting but had been unable to overcome a strong feeling, shared by everyone whose hair I had offered to cut, that I would botch the job. To my delight, Morrison agreed to let me try on condition that if I made a hopeless mess of his hair he could revenge himself on mine. It was probably owing to the fear that he might be able to claim revenge that I performed a coiffure that appeared to please him. My other client was the Carpenter, but as he was nearly bald I was not offered the same scope for artistry.

By now I had got to know my chess partner Ivan. My first impression of him was that he was eccentric. He was 20 years old, but seemed older. The most striking features of his appearance were his beard and his slight deviations from conventional style of dress: for example, a polo-necked jersey worn ashore instead of a collar and tie, and a rustic-looking walking stick. He had a very slow, thoughtful speech, was an even greater lover of long words than I, and finding someone with congenial interests would happily go on talking by the hour. He was introspective, had a vast collection of theories, and frequently made rash statements. The latter tendency I fairly quickly counteracted by pouncing on any such statement until he became more wary and more guarded in his speech. He was a devout Roman Catholic, and theology appeared to be his primary interest. He was physically clumsy with no interest in sports, but was a good walker. He certainly was good company on a long voyage.

We were glad to get through the Mozambique Channel without any signs of enemy action. We reached Aden, where we took on fuel, and then got under way again bound for Suez. During the evening watch, as we were approaching Perim lighthouse, marking the entrance to the Red Sea, we had our first experience of the heat to come. It was as though some giant had opened the door of a vast furnace. The heat struck us in waves, almost taking our breath away. The air had been damp, but this heat was dry and scorching, sucking the moisture out of everything in its path. The temperature bounded up to over 90 degrees Fahrenheit. Next morning someone with a perverted sense of humour lit the stove in the saloon, but the Chief Engineer, not to be outdone, got up in the middle of breakfast and put more coal on the fire! The energy was knocked out of us; we lay and slept, read or talked, unable to muster the will power to do anything studious or active. By day and night sweat trickled down our chests and arms, and after any exercise made us look as though we had just come out of a bath. There was a dust storm lasting a day, and when it ended there was cooler clean air, but still the blazing hot sunshine burrowed into the steel of the ship until one could feel the burning heat of the deck through thick leather soles. We were now in the zone of enemy air activity.

At Suez and the Great Bitter Lake in the Canal

While at anchor at Suez waiting to enter the Canal, we lowered one of the lifeboats and went for a sail. There was a fine breeze for sailing, but the boat made so much leeway that we had to row back against a choppy sea under the blazing sun. However, it was a welcome escape from ship's routine. Before lunch the Old Man gave a party for all the ship's officers and generously plied us with drinks and cigarettes. I admired the way he played his part as host, made everyone at home and kept the conversation flowing. At his suggestion I brought up my gramophone and played a selection of some of the lighter music, which everyone seemed to enjoy. The Captain made a short speech, thanking us all for helping to make the voyage successful and pleasant. Everyone enjoyed the gathering, which was the first time we had all been together. About a month after leaving Newcastle I had reached a state where I felt really fed up, not knowing what to do with my thoughts, restless and discontented. But now I seemed to have found my second wind for this mode of life and felt I could happily stay at sea for another month or two without going ashore.

Next day, after our wait at Suez, we were given orders to proceed along the Canal to the Great Bitter Lake to discharge our cargo at an anchorage. On our passage through the Canal we saw the vast organization for war in the forms of aerodromes, camps, guns, supply depots and prisoner of war camps. We also saw the wrecks of several ships sunk by mines in the Canal. At anchor shortly after dusk, we witnessed a fine display of searchlights. Beam after beam of light flung itself up into the air until it looked as though the framework of a great wigwam was standing over the ship. We counted over 40 lights moving across the sky, and then focusing on the same spot. Then suddenly the lights snapped out. We had no idea why.

The stevedores came aboard as soon as we anchored in the Great Bitter Lakes. They were Egyptians with little experience in cargo handling; their foremen and the man in charge were British soldiers, non-commissioned officers and Royal Engineers. To our surprise, they told us the discharging of cargo went on nearly 24 hours a day – working at night with lights on, and only turning them off when air raid warnings sounded.

The Second Mate and I went on six-hour watches, and for a week all we did was work, eat and sleep. It was really hard work, as our cargo was largely made up of heavy lifts, such as motor transport, and their discharging required our constant attention and vigilance. Our admiration for the sergeants and corporals in charge steadily increased. With completely unskilled labour whose language they hardly knew, with only the ship's derricks to lift our cargo and working 12-hour shifts, they got the job done speedily and with few accidents. We saw their officers only when they came aboard to have drinks with the Old Man.

After we had discharged the cargo, a Norwegian ship came alongside so that we could transfer the remainder of her cargo into our holds. There were many awkward heavy objects to lift, heavier than our equipment was meant to deal with. These provided us with interesting problems to solve. It was only through the superhuman efforts of the soldier foremen, and our chasing from one hatch to another, that a complete mess was avoided. By the time the loading finished I was feeling worn out and tired. Working a 12-hour day would not have been so bad if I could have slept when off duty, but the noise of winches, people shouting, the heat and the flies made sleep impossible until I was dead tired. Finally work stopped. The Second Mate and I were thankful for the rest. Even recognizing the fact that lack of sleep, the long stay aboard and the heat tended to make me irritable, I found that little injustices and annoying habits of people steadily became harder to keep in their correct perspective, and I had to fight hard to prevent them from assuming exaggerated importance.

After our cargo was loaded there was a delay before we sailed. I tried to get news of my brother, but in vain. We swam off the ship even though the water was warm and very salty. Some evenings Ivan and I played the Dvorak and Beethoven symphonies on the gramophone. The music was like balm to our tempers and mood, sweeping away all the shadows and cobwebs gathered while we had been here. In discordant contrast to the glorious music were the RAF bombers taking off from a nearby aerodrome and roaring overhead into the sunset, bent on destruction in the face of grave danger. The contrast seemed mad and incomprehensible, yet the whole world was hanging in this net made up of beauty and ugliness, love and hate, knotted together in a way that seemed to defy unravelling and consequent liberation.

Suez to Bombay

We had been in the Canal from 7 to 18 August and by the 20th we had left the Canal and were back in the Red Sea. Egypt with its sand and flies lay astern. Everyone was thankful to be on the move. The Mate became unable to keep his watch owing to semi-paralysis in one of his legs and an arm, and the Captain stood his watches. It was rotten to be ill at sea, especially in this hot weather. After paying in full our dues of sweat to the Red Sea, we were all glad to reach the relative coolness of the Arabian Sea, although we felt the heavy humidity and the swell caused by the monsoon. The sky was overcast. As we approached the Indian coast the clouds piled up and we ran into heavy rainsqualls.

This long stretch of life aboard provided me with the opportunity to observe the successive states of mind I felt on *Tahsinia*. At first there was the realization that life at sea could be very pleasant after the dirt, squalor and ugliness I met in most ports. The quiet, orderly routine of watch-keeping, the cleanliness and the great expanse of the sea and sky had a calming effect on my mood. I looked forward to the night watches when I felt able to think and see things more in perspective than I did when and living ashore and mixing in crowds. I had time to sort out and store the harvest of new impressions and ideas that I had gathered before the voyage began.

But after two or three weeks at sea the routine began to get monotonous. The loneliness of the life that I first enjoyed seemed no longer attractive. I began wanting to meet friends again, join crowds, see new faces and seek entertainment both active and passive. Restlessness set in, and it became easy to daydream. I began to wish I could stop thinking. My brain was like a mill that kept turning but had nothing to grind – a kind of hell.

There was a third state, when there set in a peace, happiness and tranquillity that I had never before encountered. I thought it must be similar to what some people experience in a monastic life. In this state I could find and develop new ideas and, when tired, my mind was able to run in neutral. This state was interrupted by our arrival at Bombay.

At Bombay

We arrived at an anchorage off Bombay harbour on 1 September. Judging by the number of ships at anchor waiting for docking space, it looked as though we would have a long wait. The crowded anchorage was due to the recent capture of Singapore by the Japanese. Many ships bound for Singapore had been rerouted to Bombay. I had never before been on a ship for three months without getting ashore. Finally the mail came aboard; my haul was four letters from home. They were terribly welcome, but for a while they made me feel very homesick. Olaf had wired home after the big battle in Egypt, and after I had worried for so long about him it was a great relief to know that he was safe and well.

We were still at anchor 12 days later, and everyone aboard had become very restless. I had managed to do a great many odd jobs, beat Ivan at chess and read a great deal. There were orders and counter-orders about our future, giving rise to speculation and rumour. Finally lighters came alongside, stevedores boarded and we commenced discharging, having been told that some of our cargo was urgently needed and that we would be shifting into the dock next day. Then a note was sent aboard saying the move had been delayed for a day or two. Everyone was fed up. We congregated on the after deck, talking and suggesting ways to pass the evening. We organized a standing high-jump competition. Later a party started in the Chief Engineer's cabin and soon everyone had had enough to drink to start singing – this went on until midnight. After yet another delay we finally docked on 15 September. Cargo work started, and I went on night work.

With the bike I kept on board it was now easy for me to get around when I went ashore. Bombay had changed since I had been there two years before. The Mission dances had been stopped, owing to free-for-alls among groups of drunks. The Mission served as a large comfortable asylum where the white inhabitants of Bombay hoped all merchant seamen would pass their spare time without causing any trouble. This may seem rather bitter, but after the hospitality and friendliness in American ports, I felt the loneliness of this place where I could not get to know families and fresh faces and could get not away from ships and seamen. It was probably due to the number of men here from the armed forces that our chances of finding any social life were reduced. Our choices of entertainment had narrowed to sightseeing, films, swimming at Breach Candy and soccer.

My bike nearly got me into trouble. One day when out cycling, I found myself in an unfamiliar quarter of the town where the streets were narrow and few Europeans were about. I had a good idea of my bearings, and in order to get back to the ship turned down a side street. I noticed four Indian police lounging on some steps, and apart from noticing their rifles, which I had not previously seen the police carrying, I took little heed of them. As I went down the side street I noticed a hush settling. I sensed a growing hostility, and felt trouble brewing. I thought it better to pretend not to notice anything, and decided to keep going at a good speed until I reached more friendly surroundings. Just then I saw a rope with a red flag being stretched across the road ahead, barring my path. As I slowed the bike, people started jeering at me. Wasting no time, I turned the bike without dismounting, and then someone started running after me. Others followed, and I heard many feet pattering after me. Someone caught hold of the bike from behind, but I pushed him off by pushing my topee (a hat used to give protection from the sun) in his face. I then accelerated in a manner that a racing cyclist would have envied. Luckily no one ahead tried to stop me, so I was able to make good my retreat at the cost possibly of a little British prestige and a three-rupee topee. I didn't grudge the price, having just read in the papers of numerous instances of mobs attacking people and putting them to death in various unpleasant ways. Possibly stopping and calmly facing the mob would have been a more dignified and equally effective method, but the potential experiment, though interesting, did not at the time appeal to me. I was not wearing my uniform, and to my knowledge did nothing to provoke the crowd, so I assumed it was an anti-British demonstration.

To get a complete change from the ship, Bombay and the noise of cargo work, I made an hour and a half journey by train and bus to Juhu Beach, which I had heard was very beautiful. I came to a long firm sandy shore lined with groves of palm trees. Heavy rollers thundered in from the sea and it and made a wonderful scene that amply repaid the trek. I undressed on the beach and went for a swim, diving into the breakers, bratting about in the shallow water and going for a run along the beach. Getting dressed, I watched the sunset playing with some dark rain clouds, for a little while turning their sombre hue into brilliant reds and gold. On the way back to the ship I had several waits for trains. I utilized the time in talking to some British servicemen who told me of their experiences in Singapore and Burma.

After we had been in port a few days the news gradually filtered through that we were not loading for home and might be stuck out East for a long time. When our next destination, Basra, became known, the gloom the news cast over the ship's company become profound, as Basra was not a port one would choose to visit. We were told that we might have to make several trips between Bombay and Basra. It took a hefty dose of grumbling to raise our spirits, which were very, very low. Because we would not get home before Christmas, I sent some presents to the family via another Anchor Line ship bound for England, under the care of the Third Engineer with whom I had sailed on the *Empire Beaver*. He kindly promised to post them when they reached England.

Bombay to Basra

At dawn on 23 September we left the dock and put to sea in a small convoy bound for Basra. I was feeling very sleepy, as I had been on duty all night. But the sea air and cool breeze were a great tonic after the dock atmosphere. For the last week in Bombay I had been feeling very poorly, first with fever and a bad cold and then weakness. I adopted the tactics of the Christian Scientists, trying to ignore the malady, which wasn't easy, and for a day or two I nearly had to give up. My illness would have thrown such a strain on the other two mates that I was glad I managed to keep going. I recovered after a day or two at sea with much sleep off watch. The illness may have been brought on by a vaccination given to everyone aboard.

Two young tank corps officers and three men who had been through the Burma campaign were passengers. One of them had with him a stock of gramophone records and a clarinet. He knew nothing about the instrument, so in the evenings I gave him lessons in the cab of one of the lorries we were carrying on the fore deck. Well out of earshot we persevered, making a few pleasant noises and many hideous ones. He said he had bought the clarinet to annoy the rest of his mess, so I assured him he would have no difficulty in carrying out his intention.

The passage was uneventful except that a soldier fell overboard from one of the troop ships. The rear ships of the column went back for him, but we didn't find out whether or not he was rescued. On entering the Persian Gulf the convoy dispersed and the race began between the ships. After a short tussle we took the lead, and by sunset we had increased it to several miles.

The Persian Gulf is reputed to be one of the hottest seas in the world, though it is drier and less oppressive than the Red Sea. On reaching the head of the Persian Gulf, at the entrance to the Shatt al Arab, we had a two-day wait at anchor. While there, the Second Engineer told us of a dream he had had: "Our ship had been sunk and the ship's company were waiting to be questioned by St Peter at the gates of Heaven. Our turn came at last, and looking down his list, he called out our names one by one. When the roll call was complete he told us that none of us was eligible for admittance and we would have to go down below. Just as we were leaving, however, he called us back to tell us that as the ship had been sunk in the middle of the Persian Gulf, orders had just arrived to send us back there, as a comparison of temperatures had shown Hell to be the cooler of the two."

Finally the Pilot boarded and took us into the broad, sluggish flowing Shatt al Arab, which is the union of the Tigris and the Euphrates rivers. At first all that was visible of the land was mud banks; then came row after row of date palms intersected by irrigation canals, where Iraqis were punting up and down among the waterways in small canoes. Wherever the irrigation stopped, the land relapsed into sandy desert. It was no wonder that some peoples worshipped the river as a God, as it represented their food and drink, their prosperity or famine. By midday the temperature had soared to 99 degrees, and going into the sunshine we could feel the heat beating down.

At Basra, Iraq

We docked in the early afternoon of 1 October. As soon as the accommodation ladder was lowered, the stevedores pounced on us to strip open the hatches and tear out the cargo. I went on night work since it was the Second Mate's choice to work during the day. I had no objection, preferring to be working when it was cool, and seeing that it did not look inviting ashore. The discharging of motor transport was hard but interesting work. The stevedores were completely unskilled and I had many interesting problems to solve using ropes, snatch blocks, the derricks and manpower. I think I enjoyed this kind of ship's work more than any other. Every day the heat was an ordeal that might easily, over time, get on my nerves and ruin my health.

During the afternoons I used to go to "The Port Club" near the docks, where there was a swimming pool. Second Lieut Mawer, who travelled with us, was a keen swimmer. The water was delightfully cool, and for two or three hours we would race, fight, lark about or laze in the pool. Then we played billiards until it was time to return to the ship for tea. In this way the days slipped by quickly and quite pleasantly.

We had two accidents and a health problem. One night I kicked over a pot of boiling water that the stevedores had left lying on the deck, and scalded my foot. The initial pain was horrible, but I kept dressing my foot and after a while the pain subsided. Ivan had a slight stroke while ashore and was laid up for a while (probably sunstroke). He returned to work but was by no means well. Just as the last of the cargo was going ashore, the Second Mate crushed the end of his finger in a wire. He went ashore to have it examined, and returned to say he had to go to a hospital to have it X-rayed and kept under observation. There was no time to replace him, so we had to sail a mate short.

Basra to Bombay

Another port lay astern, and no one regretted our departure after our six-day stay. Basra's coat of arms could well be flies and sweat on a field of sand, with possibly a date palm in one corner. We returned down the river to Abadan, where we filled up with oil fuel, and early next morning carried on. When we reached the entrance of the Shatt al Arab, a sand storm was blowing that reduced the visibility to less than quarter of a mile and made it difficult to find an anchorage. The sand added greatly to the unpleasantness of the heat by getting into our eyes and creeping into the cabins, making them look as if they hadn't been dusted for years. It made us feel dirty, parched and dried up, and though we changed into clean clothes, they had to be washed after a few hours' wear. With the absence of the Second Mate, the Old Man put me on the 12 to 4 watch while he kept the 8 to 12. It made me realize how fixed I had become in my 8 to 12 habits. For the first day I felt quite lost, having the morning free, turning in at 8 p.m. and being on watch during the middle of the night. As Second Mate I was navigator. This work was interesting and helped pass the watch.

On arriving at the entrance to the Persian Gulf, we anchored to wait for a convoy to be assembled. The convoy was made necessary by a fresh burst of activity by Japanese submarines in the Arabian Sea. Coming into the anchorage, the Old Man, unaware of the strength of the tide, attempted to pass across ahead of a naval guard ship. The current pushed us down on the guard ship, and we struck her with our port side just outside my cabin. The blow bent in the ship's side, broke our accommodation ladder and smashed the sounding boom. The guard ship appeared to have sustained no damage. I was sleeping at the time and was awakened by the sound of the collision. Half asleep, I got out of my bunk, took in at a glance what had happened, and then after deciding there was nothing I could do turned in again and went straight back to sleep. If I'd been properly awake, I certainly wouldn't have acted so casually.

On the convoy back to Bombay I became resigned to months of possibly trading between ports remarkable for mosquitoes, sand, flies and heat. I had reached a state that seemed almost emotionless, not minding particularly where we were going, how long we were to be away from home, or what happened.

At Bombay

When we arrived the Old Man went ashore, bringing back the wonderful news that we were to sail for Trinidad and then, we hoped, on to New York and home. He also brought mail, and in the seven letters for me the best news was that my brother Olaf was hoping to come home soon. While we were lying at anchor I spent time running the *Tahsinia*'s motorboat ashore, taking people on business or pleasure. It was a week before we went to our berth in the docks and began to load some manganese ore. Mr MacVicar, whom I had been with on the *Elysia*, was on another ship at Bombay. I went to see him and several other Anchor Line men who had been shipmates with me. Since I'd seen Mac last summer in New York he had married, been awarded the CBE, obtained his Master's ticket and had a daughter, so I had much to congratulate him on. I went to Breach Candy to swim, where I met Paddy, who had been an apprentice with me. He was now in the Indian Navy, and some of his friends were with him. There were two girls in his party; they were the first women that I had spoken to in four months.

I spent an interesting evening with Dr D'Monte, whom my grandparents had be-friended when he was studying medicine on a fellowship in England. They had main-tained a correspondence with him since he returned to India. My grandparents had asked me to get in touch with him and had given me his Bombay address, so I went to visit him. He was a small, thickset man with nervous gestures and rapid flowing talk that tumbled out in a jerky, impetuous manner. He talked at length about relations between India and Britain and gave a point of view different from what was heard in Britain. He felt that with the spread of literacy and transportation in India, people had enlarged the scope of their thinking about justice, trade, agriculture and politics from a local to a national level. There was a growing awareness that India was being exploited by Britain, and that self-rule was the only way of getting rid of the British Raj. British opposition to self-rule had caused Indians to focus on the evils of British rule and to turn a blind eye to any good the British had done. The British did not attend to the cry for self-rule until they panicked at the threat of losing India to Japan and having to face a full-scale revolution on top of their war problems. Then, being loathe to relinquish hold of such a lucrative investment, the British attempted to quiet India with many promises unsupported by action. The Indians suspected Britain of insincerity and false-hoods, having a wealth of historic background on which to base their suspicions.

Dr D'Monte listed some causes of anti-British feeling:

(a) Churchill had glossed over the Indian problem in his speeches, treating Indians in an unsympathetic, superior and supercilious manner.

(b) Indians felt that they had been pulled into World War II without being
consulted and were infuriated by British propaganda that would annoy any

thoughtful Indian – for example, the theme of fighting for freedom when their country did not have it.

(c) The Indian army was largely recruited from men out of work and attracted by pay that was higher than that paid for civilian work requiring equal intelligence and capability. Gandhi called India's army "an army of mercenaries", and many despised rather than admired Indian service men.

(d) Among civilians, much unrest had been caused by soaring prices, with no rise in wages to meet increased costs. The increase was due in part to profiteering, and profiteers found Britain a useful scapegoat behind which to hide. In places there were acute shortages of necessities such as rice, sugar, wheat and kerosene oil.

(e) Many believed that the Indian problem was being unfairly presented in England and that strict censorship was in force governing news leaving India.

Trouble was inevitable when the judicial and police organizations were closely allied. The police, in curbing free speech, were hushing up cases with Gestapo-like methods.

I was impressed by how succinctly Dr D'Monte presented his views.

One of the letters I received in Bombay was from Janet. I had first met her three years before on *Elysia*, where I had fallen in love with her. A year later we had met again at Karachi. Since then our correspondence had been decreasing both in length and in frequency. Over time my feelings for Janet had slowly changed. Seeing her for only a few days, I had idealized her. In one of my first letters to her I wrote that "time does many things to us for which we are not responsible". This seemed to have happened, and I no longer felt in love with Janet.

I had a fair idea from her letters that she had also experienced this change. Her letter told me that she and her family were probably moving to Bombay. I went to the Naval Office, learned that the family was in Bombay, and obtained their address and phone number. I phoned to arrange a meeting with Janet. Her parents had just gone out when I arrived. I encouraged her to talk about herself, as she had put little in her last letters. The talk throughout was almost conventional, either from intent, reserve or shyness, but I soon became sure she had passed through the same change of feelings as I had. I think we were quite glad when her parents returned, as we were beginning to run short of small talk and news, and had avoided sharing our feelings. The Mackays were very good at light conversation, and talk flowed evenly and pleasantly. Janet and I seemed to have made a silent agreement to the effect: "What's the use of getting to know each other again, only to say good-bye and have further long separations with so much uncertainty about the future? Time would be the most tactful helper in finishing this off." I said good-bye. A few days later I spent another evening ashore but did not go to see Janet again.

On 27 October we left the dock and went out into the harbour, where we lay at anchor for a week. The Second Mate we had left behind in Basra rejoined us. Besides running people ashore in the ship's motorboat, I often went sailing in the late afternoon when the breeze was strongest. The boat would not sail well to windward, so we would sail for a while and then put on the engine and steer to windward until we made up lost ground. Not very seamanlike, but most enjoyable. I taught Morrison enough so that he became a competent helper. Sailing made me feel happier than I had been for a long time.

Bombay to Lorenzo Marques

We put to sea on 3 November. During the passage to Lorenzo Marques the cooler weather was a great joy to all of us. We had warm sunshine tempered by cool trade winds, and a sky with white gliding cumulus clouds. Because the decks were now clear of cargo we were able to play deck tennis. Some of the crew had learned to play chess, and there was a growing circle of enthusiastic players. The book *War and Peace* was the perfect companion for a long voyage. Since leaving Bombay I felt that I had had a holiday, leaving the ship for an hour a day and going to Russia where, with Tolstoy as a guide, I went through the Napoleonic war and entered the houses of the Russian aristocrats to get to know Andrew Bokenski, Pierre, the Rostous and many others.

We saw no enemy action during those days, but there was considerable U-boat activity reported round the South African coast and the Mozambique Channel. The Old Man ordered extra precautions, such as doubling up on the lookouts and zigzagging the ship. We were easily visible at night because of a full moon. As we approached Lorenzo Marques, a neutral port on the African side of the Mozambique Channel, the number of submarine reports increased. When we picked up the Pilot, he told us a Greek ship had been sunk a few hours previously within a few miles of the port. Several other ships were lost in the same place after our arrival.

After lying at anchor for a weekend, we went to a dock where we took on oil fuel, water, and supplies. We had only one evening ashore, where we passed the time walking around town, drinking coffee at cafés while watching people, and going to a good comedy film, *The Return of Topper*.

We were told that the submarine blockade had become so effective here that nearly every ship that had left the previous week had been sunk. As a result the port was closed and we were delayed. Lorenzo Marques was known to be rife with enemy agents, and probably they kept the U-boats in touch with shipping movements. The enemy agents probably had little difficulty in getting information from sailors when they went ashore because there was little for them to do except drink and go to brothels where they could be persuaded to give it away. This problem had been addressed by the British and Allies in other ports, where seaman's clubs had been established. These provided attractive entertainment, and local people who attended the clubs could be carefully checked. The expense of running such a club would have been far less than that of replacing ships lost by careless talk.

We had been hoping for the arrival of mail forwarded from Durban, but none came.

Lorenzo Marques to Georgetown, British Guiana

We slipped out of the harbour on 1 December in company with some other ships and steamed southward, hugging the coast line so as to remain within neutral waters as long as possible. We had a British destroyer with us for a few hours, but she left when it grew dark. During the evening we were surprised to see searchlights far to the eastward and a ship showing lights. Probably the lights came from a Portuguese gunboat that the Pilot had told us had put to sea looking for survivors of a ship that had been sunk a few hours before we weighed anchor.

We went far south of Africa to avoid submarines, entering the "Roaring Forties" where winds often reached strong gale force and rarely died away. A heavy sea was running, and a huge swell slowed us down to half our normal speed. The temperature fell to the 40s. We were all feeling the cold.

One morning when the stewards were called, the bunk of the Captain's "Tiger'" (steward) had not been slept in and there was no sign of its occupant. His mates searched the ship with growing alarm until forced to realize that he was no longer on board. Saturday evening had been a wild night, the ship was rolling heavily, and the Steward must have fallen overboard. The darkness, the wind and the sea hid his disappearance; no one heard a shout, or saw any unusual sign. He had spent the evening in the forecastle and was last seen as he went aft to his own cabin. The man who came to the wheel at 10 o'clock was rather drunk; his condition was the only indication that a party had been going on in the forecastle.

Over the radio we heard that *Cromer*, a minesweeper, had been lost. The tragedy of that brief statement struck home for me with full force. Mr Martin was aboard the *Cromer*, and he and his family were neighbours and close friends of our family.

This long passage was a good time for studying for the Mate's certificate. If I kept to two hours' study a day, it gave me the weekend clear; but if the flesh was weak, I had to make up lost time studying during the weekend. When I grew restless my thoughts often flew home to friends and activities. The voyage had become so long that these thoughts were worn threadbare and no longer satisfied. Sometimes a wave of homesickness would sweep over me until I could catch hold of some occupation to distract my attention. These included playing in a chess tournament, listening to music on the gramophone, deck tennis or reading.

I usually worked in harmony with the Mate, although sometimes I had to strongly suppress the desire to be rude to him because his manner irritated me. He was good at his work, but seemed insensitive in dealing with people and tended to rub them up the wrong way. He had a dread lest his dignity might suffer, and the topic of conversation he most often pursued was himself. A sense of humour might have tempered these two traits, but I found by sad experience that he saw humour only in the stupidity of others, and then used it as a pointer towards his own efficiency. I avoided argument with him, as I found it unprofitable and aggravating owing to the superior and dogmatic attitude he adopted on such occasions.

My opinion of the Mate dropped as the voyage proceeded, but with the Second Mate the opposite occurred. My first impression of the Second Mate was unfavourable; labels such as "dour", "boorish" and "pushing" might easily have been attached to him. His eyes were the most attractive part of him, as they showed keen intelligence and humour (a blessed virtue), and deep down lurked a twinkle of mischief and fun. Our outlook on life and our interests hardly overlapped, and it was a long time before I found how to get on with him. It was to use his style of humour, which brought out his best side; he could then be most amusing company. He frequently crossed swords with the Old Man, and not having much to fall back on outside his work, he nursed his grievances until they became almost obsessions.

We returned to the tropics again as we headed northward in the South Atlantic. In contrast to the traditional cold snowy Christmas scene at home, we had sea, blue sky, hot steel decks and figures clad in shorts and sandals. On Christmas Eve I felt in the mood for carols. Not being able to find people to listen, I rendered "O Come All Ye Faithful" down the wireless room ventilator to Senior Sparks, who was polite enough to say he enjoyed it.

On Christmas Day I forswore my usual rule of not thinking too much about home and friends, and passed the morning watch speculating on their probable activities. I enlisted the services of the Fourth Engineer and Fifth Engineer to fulfil the Christmas tradition of serving the stewards their dinner. Then activities moved to the deck tennis court, where we had some enjoyable matches. Exercise having been taken, the party dispersed to lie down and relax. After tea, Ivan and I were in the early stages of a gramophone concert when the Chief broke in to commandeer our services for carol singing at a party in the Second Mate's cabin. Everyone at the party had drunk sufficient to lubricate their vocal chords thoroughly; we attacked with vigour all the carols we could remember.

At Georgetown, British Guiana

We reached Georgetown, on 28 December after a 28-day passage; by New Year's Eve we were tied up waiting to load a cargo of sugar. As we were a Scottish ship, the New

Year was considered a more important festival than Christmas. Being on night duty, I had expected a quiet evening aboard, with the crew making merry ashore; but it was not to be. The New Year came in at home at 7.15 p.m. local time, and a party collected to hear the hour tolled by Big Ben through the wireless. It brought forth a spirited rendering of Auld Lang Syne, with much shaking of hands and exchanging of good wishes by all. The Chief, who excelled at leading singsongs, soon had everyone singing. The Old Man and a skipper from another British ship joined us for a while. Sentimental speeches followed, until politeness could no longer restrain the urge to sing.

The gaiety and rowdiness increased in proportion to the amount drunk. It was noticeable that while at the beginning of the party it was difficult to persuade people to sing solos, towards the end it was difficult to stop them. We drank toasts to the folks at home, the Old Man and the Chief, but rather to my surprise no mention was made of war or peace. The members of the party reiterated their intention of going ashore, and some of the less drunk finally went. Others remained on board singing, until they were helped to their cabins and assisted in undressing. Then the ship was quiet. The ship's night watchman, a lad of 18, lay asleep drunk; the gunner on watch had deserted his post and was ashore in search of pleasure, and only the mosquitoes and the shore guards remained.

We should have started loading sugar as soon as we arrived, but the rainy season fulfilled its name and the rain poured down, preventing any work as moisture was harmful to the sugar. The stevedores worked an eight-hour day, no night work, and had two days' holiday for the New Year, so for the first time this trip we weren't overworked while in port. Most evenings that I went ashore I spent dancing at the USO (the Americans' organization for entertaining their servicemen). It was a fine club, with a large ballroom cum theatre and a large cafe. There was an excellent band, the floor wasn't too crowded and there was no shortage of partners. The girl I first danced with taxed my powers of light conversation because I could not find any mutual interests. Her only interests that I could find were going to parties and playing hockey. Eventually she left, and after that I played safe and only had one dance with each partner.

An interesting feature of Georgetown was the result of generations of interbreeding between the African, British, Chinese, Dutch, Indian and Portuguese. The original colonists were Portuguese. Then the colony was taken over by the British, who brought in freed African slaves, Indians and some Chinese to work on the sugar plantations. With so much mixing of races, there seemed to be no basis for race prejudice. The exception appeared to be the Portuguese, who kept more to themselves and closely chaperoned their daughters. I felt that the most beautiful women were a mixture of African and Chinese.

Georgetown was built at sea level, with dikes to keep out the sea. Irrigation and drainage canals criss-crossed the streets, giving an effect similar to that of a Dutch town. The town's main charm lay in its detachment from the outside world. It was almost untouched by the war, and the life and customs of the town all seemed old fashioned, slow and a pleasant change from other ports. At a dance, an Englishman asked me if I was interested in riding. Finding that I was, he offered to lend me his horse. It was too good a chance to miss. The following day I cycled out to the hotel he owned and found the horse ready and waiting. Luckily for me she behaved beautifully, and although very energetic had no bad habits. Unfortunately, since it was high tide, I was unable to gallop on the sands. The coast was infested with mosquitoes that rose in clouds as we passed. Afterwards my host invited me in for a drink and we swapped reminiscences of home.

Guiana to New York via Trinidad

We were unable to load a full load cargo of sugar at Georgetown because the draft of the ship would have been too great to get over the shallows at the entrance to the port. So we made the short passage to Trinidad, where we loaded the remainder of the sugar and waited for a convoy to assemble. On 24 January we put to sea as part of a large convoy. Our passage to New York was uneventful. The two apprentices and I took advantage of some glorious weather to thoroughly overhaul all the life-saving gear in the lifeboats before we entered the cold weather north of the Gulf Stream. After we reached the Ambrose Light off New York Harbour, we crept up the harbour in raw, wet weather to dock on 5 February at pier 97, close to the heart of New York City.

At New York

It seemed ages since I had been at a port where I had friends and there were theatres, concerts and opera. We were all excited and eager to go ashore. Officials came aboard to take our fingerprints and issue identification cards and passes. They told us that a visa for the ship had to be sent from Washington before we could go ashore. Two days dragged past while we prowled around the ship like caged tigers, our bars being made of red tape. No one could settle down; we just sat round in the saloon, idly talking. If any official came on board we would watch him like hungry dogs waiting for a meal. Finally we were told the visa had been waived and we could go ashore.

When we reached New York, the length, uncertainties, and loneliness of the voyage on *Tahsinia* had put me in a state bordering on depression and cynicism. The kindness I experienced there while ashore restored me to my more usual cheerful and optimistic state. The McCulloughs, whom I had got to know on a previous voyage, took me into their home and made me a part of their family life. Whenever I could get a night ashore I stayed at their large, comfortable house. Mrs McCullough entertained me royally, taking me to plays, concerts, operas and restaurants. Sometimes I would go to the

Merchant Navy club, where the hostess, Mrs Wilson, provided access to dances and obtained theatre tickets for me, other members of the crew and our friends. I went to several dances with Midge, whom I had met on a previous visit to New York – a tall English girl, a good conversationalist who worked in a decoding section of the British Admiralty office.

Several years earlier in England I had met Ursula, a Jewish refugee from Germany who had moved on to New York, where she was training as a nurse. As I had her address, I looked her up and spent considerable time with her. She told me that if she had been allowed to remain in her old way of life in Germany she would have had no need to work; after completing an expensive and carefully sheltered education, she would probably have done nothing useful but spend money and seek pleasure while waiting for a wealthy husband to come along. Instead, she now would have to earn her living as a nurse. There were also drastic changes in her father's way of life: from being the manager of one of the largest cotton mills in Europe to being a small poultry farmer in New Jersey. She believed that she and her father were happier now than they used to be.

With severe food rationing in Britain, we all wanted to buy food to take home. The crew had compiled a joint list of all our requirements, and we obtained everything through our agents. When the food arrived, the task of sorting it into individual lots and working out everyone's share of the cost was quite an undertaking.

Two days after docking the temperature started falling, and by nightfall the thermometer read 2 degrees Fahrenheit. The Third Engineer and I were out during the night trying to prevent the pipelines from freezing up. The following day we woke up shivering with the cold. The heating system on the ship being totally inadequate for such an extreme, we gathered in the saloon, falling over each other (metaphorically) in our efforts to stoke the stove. The engineers raided our drawers for surplus jerseys and scarves and we went about weighed down with clothes. Despite our efforts all the water pipes on the ship froze, including the hot water circulating pipe. Later, using a blowlamp, I spent several hours thawing them out.

We were to load sections of an invasion-landing barge on deck, but were delayed by the cold. The barges onto which they had been loaded were frozen in the ice. Finally the tugs broke the ice and brought the barges alongside us. A large floating crane quickly placed the barge sections on our deck, and shore experts lashed down the sections with heavy wires. Little was happening aboard *Tahsinia*, and the expected day of departure passed. We lived from day to day, always expecting to sail the next day. The extension of our stay was unexpected and welcome, but it prevented our making any shore plans. By the time we sailed, the process of saying good-bye to friends ashore and then turning up the next day became quite monotonous. Finally we were sent to an anchorage off City Island to wait, because the convoy that we were to sail with was full up. While we waited at the anchorage, the damage to the frozen pipes was repaired.

We got orders on short notice to shift to an anchorage off Staten Island only an hour or two before the Pilot came aboard. The Old Man and Ivan were ashore, unaware of our shift on short notice, so were left behind. When Ivan returned to City Island he found *Tahsinia* had gone. To add to his difficulties, he had spent almost all his money, so he phoned my friend Midge for help. She told him to come and see her, lent him money, gave him dinner, entertained him with gramophone records and generally fussed over him while she found out where the ship was. Next day she got him back to *Tahsinia*. The Captain had little difficulty in rejoining the ship with the help of the ship's agent.

New York to Halifax

We put to sea in a convoy on 27 February. The following morning the weather was fine, the sea calm, our destination Liverpool, and we seemed all set for the last lap of the long voyage, but it was not to be. Because the convoy was too large, the Commodore started to issue orders to some ships to go to Halifax. We watched anxiously as the numbers of the ships to leave the convoy were given by flag signals from the commodore ship. Eventually our number was hoisted. The additional delay was heartily cursed by the ship's company, but being selfish, I was quite pleased, as it increased my chance of having sufficient sea time to go up for my Mate's certificate by the time we got home. As we approached the position where we should have broken away from the convoy, heavy rain set in that later changed to a dense fog. It was too dangerous to disperse, so we stayed with the convoy. We spent the next two days peering into the swirling cold, damp fog looking for ships in the convoy, and listening for the mournful cry of ships' whistles sending out their numbers.

When the fog cleared we were 300 miles east of Halifax, and on leaving the convoy had to retrace part of our route, in company with the other unfortunate ships. The first night of the return trip was most unpleasant. The temperature was 21 degrees Fahrenheit and we were punching into a moderate gale and shipping heavy seas. Clouds of spray deluged the bridge, the wheelhouse windows were crusted with thick ice and there was nowhere to shelter from the elements. The water froze as it landed on deck and on the bridge we had to hold on to avoid slipping. When I came below at midnight I had to stand in front of the fire in the saloon to allow the ice to thaw from my oilskins, and then wash thick salt from my face. Rarely had a bunk appeared so comfortable and inviting.

When we reached Halifax on 6 March, we learned that there would be a several-day stay. Money and passes were brought aboard by the Old Man, and by evening most of the crew were ashore. I was on duty, so had a quiet evening aboard writing and reading. In really cold weather the saloon was the one warm place on the ship and the coal stove gave it a cosy atmosphere. One day we negotiated the distribution to the crew of woollen comforters, given by the Canadian Red Cross. For the remainder of our stay the time slipped past pleasantly, as there were various odd jobs we needed to do for the ship that kept me busy. The only galling part of our stay in Halifax was that we could have stayed another 10 days in New York and been home just as soon. Also we would have saved fuel and effort, and decreased the risk to the ship.

Halifax to Liverpool

We left Halifax on 11 March in a small convoy. Hardly had we formed up when fog set in that lasted all night. It showed no signs of thinning, leaving us with the problem of finding the main part of the convoy coming up from New York. To make a rendez-vous in clear weather we could sight other ships many miles away, but in dense fog the chances of meeting were slight, with no way of finding ships until we heard their whistles, and no chance of fixing our own position by celestial observations. Going on soundings and dead reckoning, we tackled the problem, and late that afternoon, more by luck than good judgement, we heard the whistles of the New York section of the main convoy.

The fog lasted for the next day or two, and we hung on to the ships as best we could. When at last the fog cleared, we began getting into our proper stations. The Commodore signalled that enemy subs were in close proximity and kept us going as fast as the slowest ship was able to steam. Then we started encountering pancake and flow ice, some of which was thick enough to damage a ship, but the Commodore wouldn't reduce speed. All we could do was to pick our way through the leads in the ice and try to keep up with the convoy.

Eventually, to our relief, the flow ice disappeared, but next to worry about were some small icebergs that, if hit, could sink us. During the day they were easily sighted, but they were very difficult to see at night. Sometimes the escort vessels would flash their searchlights on them to indicate their presence. The weather, which had been fine for a short time, took a turn for the worse and we began getting heavy snow flurries that would last up to half an hour, reducing the visibility to little more than a ship's length. We kept driving on, with icebergs still passing at frequent intervals. It was taking a huge risk, but it seemed that the best way to avoid U-boats was to follow the craziest route imaginable. All we could do was take a good look round when it cleared, and while the snow was thick trust to luck, hoping to see the bergs before hitting them. As we got further north and east the bergs became less frequent, but the ones we sighted were massive brutes well over a hundred feet high and several hundred yards across. After a week of such weather we finally got away from the ice and extreme cold.

Life aboard was not very pleasant during this really cold, rough weather. The fresh water supply froze up and only one tap kept running, so all water for washing had to be pumped up by hand and carried in buckets, making washing and laundry most unpleasant. The drains got clogged up with ice, so all water had to be thrown overboard. *Tahsinia* was almost as dirty a sea boat as the *Beaver*, when loaded and in bad weather. For several nights my bunk was soaked, as seas could not be dissuaded from finding their way in through a vent above my bunk. The last half of the crossing was less eventful; we saw no sign of enemy activity. One night we ran into a terrific beam swell, and *Tahsinia* rolled her bulwarks right under. We rolled through 70 degrees, which was pretty wicked for a loaded ship. Luckily the lashing on the deck cargo withstood the strain.

We reached Liverpool on 30 March. Owing to the delays on the voyage, my sea time for the Mate's certificate was complete. The Mate and Second Mate went home on leave, but I remained with the ship for a month while she discharged her cargo and went into dry dock. Then we took her to Barrow in Furness to be fitted with nets that could be lowered down along the sides of the ship to intercept torpedoes. During that time I had many pleasant experiences, such as visiting friends in Liverpool, exploring the southern end of the Lake District on my bike and staying a weekend with relatives. Having been away for almost a year, I was impatient to get home. At the end of April I left the *Tahsinia* and went to my parents, who had moved from Paisley to a new home that overlooked the Holy Loch on the Firth of Clyde.

On the voyage after I left the *Tahsinia*, two submarines attacked her 360 miles west of Ceylon (Sri Lanka). After being hit by four torpedoes, she was sunk by gunfire. None of the crew was lost. They took to the lifeboats, and the one with an engine towed the others for a day and a half until fuel ran out. They then continued by sail and were picked up by a British ship, having covered 300 miles.

CHAPTER 5

Kelmscott

Voyage 1 – October to December 1943

After leaving *Tahsinia* in May 1943 I returned to my parents' new home in Kilmun, the house my father had bought when he retired. Throughout May I enjoyed sailing my dinghy, helping my father with the garden and going for long walks with my dog Nansen. It was a welcome change from life at sea. From the end of May to the beginning of August I studied at the Glasgow Technical College for my First Mate's certificate. While I was there, the King and Queen visited the merchant navy officers at the college. We lined up in a hallway. When they were walking past, the Queen stopped and asked me what kinds of ships I had been on and where I had been on them. They came to the college in recognition of the heavy loss of merchant seamen owing to enemy action. In early August I sat the week-long written and aural examinations and passed in all subjects.

I reported the results to the Marine Superintendent of the Anchor Line, and after a few days he offered me a Third Mate's berth on a new ship being built to carry newsprint from Canada and Newfoundland to Britain. I had hoped for a First Mate's berth. I learned that I was not qualified because it was company policy that every First Mate had to have a Master's certificate in case, in the event of a mishap, he had to take over the Master's position. The position I was offered paid an extra 50% bonus above normal wages. This would give me more pay than Second Mates on any other type of ship, and cargoes of newsprint meant that I would get home every two to three months, so I accepted the offer. Since the ship wasn't finished, it would give me more time at home.

Delays in completing the new ship kept me until the middle of October. During this time I was a relieving officer on two ships in Glasgow. The Marine Superintendent then told me that when the *Kelmscott,* another of their newsprint ships, returned it would

The Kelmscott, *c.1960 (Reproduced from the Manchester Ship Canal Company photographic archives with kind permission from Greater Manchester County Record Office)*

Kelmscott – *loading newsprint*

need a Second Mate and I could have the position. This was preferable to the earlier offer of a Third Mate's position, so I was delighted. I would still get the 50% bonus. I bought more gold braid to make a second stripe on my uniform. On 15 October a wire arrived telling me to join the *Kelmscott* at London,

When I joined my new ship she was only a few months old, an excellent age for a ship. She was old enough for the equipment and stores to have been sorted out and put in their appointed positions, and for the initial mistakes and deficiencies to have been rectified, yet not old enough for equipment to be worn out and the accommodations to have become shabby and dirty. The ship suffered from wartime restrictions, but the accommodation was comfortable. My first few days were fully occupied in getting to know the ship, picking up the threads of work, organizing the chart room and navigation gear, meeting the ship's company and, when off duty, going to the theatre and seeing my sister who was living in London.

I helped the Captain sign on the crew and then returned to the ship. That afternoon orders arrived putting our sailing date forward two days. To comply, a hectic rush ensued, recalling the crew and preparing for sea. Every night I was in London the air raid sirens sounded and German raiders were overhead. Nothing except shrapnel dropped near us. On 23 October we left the quay and started down the Thames.

London to Saint John, New Brunswick

On our passage up the east coast, German E-boats (small, fast torpedo boats) attacked our convoy. Because we were near the centre of the convoy we heard the gunfire but saw no E-boats. It wasn't until a day or two later that we learned the details on the wireless: over 30-E boats had attacked, and in a running action with our escort lasting five hours the Germans had suffered heavy losses.

As Second Mate I was now on the 12 to 4 watch so had to completely reorganize my daily routine. For the first few nights I found getting up at 11.45 p.m. to go on watch most disagreeable. Coming out from a nice warm bunk onto a cold, draughty bridge at midnight was like getting into a cold bath. For the first few minutes I would gasp with the cold, but as the watch progressed I became more accustomed to the rigours of the night. For a while I wasted time by not making a daily plan of what to do when off watch. I had found that if I made a daily plan of activities I would then go ahead and get on with the allotted tasks, while without a programme I tended to drift and have nothing to show for the day. Previously my main responsibility off watch had been looking after the lifeboats and all life-saving equipment; now I was the main ship's navigator, a far more interesting job.

After rounding the north coast of Scotland, we steamed south and joined an Atlantic convoy. At this time of year in the North Atlantic the sun was reluctant to appear, making it difficult to fix our position. Devoted sun worshippers would have been proud of the Captain and me in our assiduity to be in attendance on the sun. At the first hint of a visit from the sun, one of our two cadets (this term was now used instead of apprentice) was dispatched post haste to summon us. We went into instant action, and woe betide anyone who got in our way during our charge up the steps to the bridge and chart room. Grabbing our sextants, we would storm out of the wheelhouse onto the bridge, where we generally found that the sun had, at the last moment, found a cloud to hide behind. This performance, although containing an element of humour, became tiresome with frequent repetition.

The weather deteriorated as we steamed westward. The *Kelmscott* rolled so heartily that after a few days we grew very tired of her movements. I didn't get seasick but reached a stage where if the rolling did not stop I wanted to scream. As we neared Halifax, a south-easterly gale sprang up. Throughout the night we lay hove to outside the harbour with *Kelmscott* making crab-like progress up and down and around the outer fairway buoy to the port's entry. Next morning the wind dropped, and we proceeded to our berth where we took on fuel.

During the outward passage, the Second Engineer's hand was badly lacerated in the engine governor. The weather was too bad for a doctor to be sent across from one of the escorts; the Chief Steward treated the wound, with the help of advice signalled over by Morse from the escort. As soon as we docked, the Second Engineer was taken ashore to the hospital. We remained only a few hours in port and then continued on the last lap of our passage. A night or two later, amidst sleet and snow squalls, we docked at Saint John, New Brunswick.

At Saint John, New Brunswick

In the first few days at Saint John I spent all my spare time shopping for people at home and for myself. Compared with those in the UK the shops were well stocked, but I had some difficulty in finding what I had been asked to buy. I hoped we would get back home for Christmas, and looked for a chicken that I could keep fresh in the ship's refrigerator. After I explained my need to the shopkeeper, he produced and sold me one of his best chickens. With severe rationing in place, I was bringing home a real treat. There were several shops that sold toys, and I had great fun wandering round trying to look grown-up and rather bored but experiencing great difficulty in preventing myself from playing with the many tempting games and models on display. When I was tired of shopping I would go to a gramophone shop, where the girl in charge invited me to come in any time to listen to records even if I had no intention of buying.

In the centre of Saint John there was a hospitality centre but for the first few days I didn't go there. Eventually, however, I met the secretary of the hospitality centre, who introduced me to a woman who was at the hub of musical activity in Saint John.

This led to several musical evenings at her home, where I was able to join in with my clarinets.

I saw newsprint loaded for the first time. Each roll was about eight feet long and three feet in diameter; they fitted together in tiers in the holds. The longshoremen were skilled in this work, and on duty there was little for me to do. On previous ships, where we carried many kinds of cargo destined for several ports, we had to make detailed plans of where the cargo was stowed, and be concerned about cargo being broached. Now this was unnecessary.

A new experience for me was dealing with the rise and fall of the tide. We were in the Bay of Fundy, which has one of the greatest tidal ranges in the world. Tied up to a dock, we had to be vigilant in slacking or tightening our mooring ropes to prevent them from breaking at low tide, and to keep us close to the dock at high tide.

The huge tidal range at the mouth of the Saint John River gave rise to the remarkable phenomenon of the reversing falls. I went to see them at different stages of the tide. At low water there was a waterfall from the river down into the sea; at mid tide large ships could pass the spot because the water level in the river and the sea was the same; and at high tide the water fell from the sea into the river.

Saint John to Manchester

Our homeward passage in December was memorable for the ferocity of a gale that struck a day or two after we sailed, completely breaking up our convoy. We were out of touch with the convoy for half a day with a few other ships that were hove to, plunging about like animals trying to escape from a trap and often hidden behind great clouds of spray. It seemed as though the line between sea and sky had disappeared and the ship was battling in a transitional medium of howling wind, slashing spray and rain which had lost its sense of direction, not knowing whether it was driving towards earth or sky. Luckily the newsprint we were carrying did not put the ship down to her marks (the maximum legal draught) so we had sufficient reserve buoyancy to ride even heavy seas without shipping too much water. We felt sorry for the naval escort of corvettes and destroyers that were taking a terrible pounding from the sea, and where water in their accommodation must have been a greater issue than it was for us.

Our two cadets were a difficult problem. The indenture system I had experienced as an apprentice had ended, and now our cadets had taken a six-month course at the Nautical School in Glasgow before joining us. On the *Tahsinia*, although the cadets were far from clever, by the end of a year they were well on the road to becoming useful junior officers. On this ship I feared that we had failed in our training of these cadets. The older of the two boys, Hansen, was 17, had a pleasing appearance and was light on his feet. He was the more conscientious of the two and had, I suspect, a rather sensitive nature easily hurt by sarcasm or being shouted at. He showed little initiative or aptitude at his work; his speech was slovenly; he had a poor memory and great difficulty in expressing himself. We mates knew this and tried to be patient with him and not blame him for what he was incapable of learning. Unfortunately he got on people's nerves and in consequence sometimes got shouted at.

The younger boy, Taggart, also 17, was less limited than Hansen, but more apt to dodge work and tell lies. He didn't realize that to be a good liar required a good memory and intelligence. He had a rather grubby, ugly appearance, and spoke with a broad Glasgow accent; I'm afraid I had difficulty liking him. On several occasions the cadets were given lectures and demonstrations on how to keep their cabin and clothes clean, but one day the Mate had found they had no clean clothes, all their dirty things were strewn round the cabin, and cigarette ash, papers and mess were everywhere. Taggart and Hansen were always bickering and quarrelling, and Taggart was apt to bully Hansen and take advantage of his low intelligence. Neither of them had any hobby or interest that we could discover. I encouraged them to study and read but had little success.

The problem that confronted us was this: should we keep the boys on the ship and by constant persuasion, help, threats and tuition try to make something out of what was poor-quality material, or should we get rid of them and allow two of the hundreds of intelligent and keen boys waiting for a chance to come to sea an opportunity to fulfil their ambition? The Old Man, First Mate, Third Mate and I discussed the problem. We decided to warn them that unless they showed more interest in their work they would have to leave. We would ask Captain Bowie, our Marine Superintendent, to talk to them when we got back to England, and then give them the next voyage to see if they could make good.

After the gale, the homeward passage was uneventful although there was considerable enemy activity close to us. When we reached Liverpool we received orders to anchor before proceeding to Manchester, and for days we lay idle. Most of the crew welcomed the delay as it increased our chance of having Christmas at home. Others were restless, unable to settle to any occupation. Eventually orders to proceed were Morsed across to us, and we crept up the channel towards the Manchester Ship Canal, steering compass courses and trying to see through the fog that was blowing out to sea from the land. We took two days going up the canal, tying up at night.

At Manchester the unloading of newsprint went smoothly, and I was able to get ashore frequently. On 19 December the Halle orchestra was to perform the *Messiah*. Malcolm Sargent was to conduct the orchestra and choir. I was able to go, and although all booked seats were sold I got into the back of the vast hall at Belle Vue. The performers were in the ring where the Christmas circus was held. After the concert I went round to see a friend, Arthur Percival, the deputy leader of the orchestra, who kindly invited me home for tea. On the way he told me that the previous year the *Messiah* had been performed at the same place, and some elephants were stabled backstage where the orchestra gathered during the intervals. A cockney horn player gazed at the elephants for a long time in silence and then, sensing the somewhat strong odour which came from the beasts, remarked, "They give you quite the atmosphere of the manger, don't they, blokes?"

I travelled north on leave the following evening, arrived at Glasgow at 1.30 a.m., and walked the seven miles to my previous home in Paisley to sleep at a friend's house. The following day I went on by train and steamer to my parents' new home at Kilmun on the Firth of Clyde, arriving in the afternoon. The views of the Firth had changed since my last leave. The mountains were snow clad, and lower down the colouring was more sombre though none the less beautiful than in summer.

I had expected a quiet Christmas, but it turned out to be one of the most social and enjoyable leaves I had experienced in a long time. Our family organized a party at our house and I was surprised by the guests' slowness at a game that entailed discovering, by questioning, the name of a famous person pinned to their backs. The Minister took twenty minutes before finding out he was David Livingstone, but the time wasn't altogether wasted because the following Sunday he brought Livingstone into his sermon. On Christmas Eve, the dance in the village hall was great. There was much genuine enjoyment, good spirits (don't misconstrue) and friendliness, as well as excellent dancing – the number of men and women was nearly even so few people had to sit out. Later in the evening some happy drunks rolled in and started singing carols between the dances. Once they started, everyone joined in.

I gave Mother the chicken that I had bought in Canada. She asked Mr McKintyre, the butcher, if he would truss the bird. He agreed, saying that he hadn't seen such a fine chicken since the beginning of the war. This was no mere politeness because for the next day or two every customer who entered his shop was introduced to the bird and shown all its good points. We had Christmas dinner on the 24th, because I was afraid I might be recalled to the ship that night. However, no summons came until the following Monday, when I left by the last boat and went on to by train to Glasgow, where I spent the evening seeing friends before returning on the night train to the *Kelmscott* at Manchester.

Voyage 2 – December 1943 to March 1944

The discharging of the newsprint cargo was in progress when I got back aboard. I had a conference with the Mate, getting acquainted with the work in progress and what had to be done while he was on leave. The following 10 days in Manchester passed pleasantly: I visited friends ashore, and found the work on board interesting and plentiful. Before sailing, as usual, we took on ballast.

Manchester to St John's, Newfoundland, via Bell Island

During the passage we encountered a week of bad weather such as I had never seen before; even the Old Man said he could not remember the likes of it. The barometer bounced up and down at a speed of sometimes half an inch in four hours, and fresh gales swept down on us alternately from south and west. The wind set up a precipitous, confused swell, which threw us about with extreme violence. It was only possible to sleep when we were so dog tired that we could shut out the violent movement and the crash and rattle of the ship's goods and chattels careening madly about the accommodation and decks. No amount of wedging and lashing seemed to be able to restrain them. A raft was lost over the side; the pounding of the seas started leaks in No. 1 hold, and two of the ships in the convoy broke up and sent out SOS messages. On one of those stormy nights, gunfire from one of the escorts on our side of the convoy indicated an attack by U-boats. The action lasted several hours, but the following day we learned nothing of the result. At times like this, the weather seemed a greater menace than the danger of enemy action.

When the wind was from the south we got driving rain, and when the wind veered to the north-west it turned into hail and snow squalls. Any occupations except reading and trying to sleep were almost impossible, yet the cook with great gallantry kept to his work under appalling conditions to provide us with hot food. Meals were an exercise in balance. By now everyone had grown very tired of the incessant movement. The cheerfulness and good humour maintained by everybody was outstanding, with the most annoying incidents being laughed at. The great longing now was to have *Kelmscott* on an even keel and calm. The clinometer in the chartroom showed that we were rolling through 78 degrees.

On the last two days of the outward passage the weather moderated, but the sea, refusing to lie quiet, would every now and again throw the ship into a sudden vicious roll as if finding vast amusement at our discomfort. Our first port of call was Bell Island, off the northern tip of Newfoundland, where we were to discharge our ballast. On the day of our arrival I went out on deck to find great cliffs towering over the ship as we approached a pier. The arrival of our ship caused quite a stir, as we were the first since before Christmas. The island's only industry was mining, which provided little employment as only two shifts a week were being worked. Before the war they had exported large quantities of iron ore to Germany. Now this market had closed and the island was hard hit. During our stay the ship provided employment for about a hundred men, and we were constantly being asked whether there were any vacancies in the crew that they could fill.

The first evening we were alongside I went ashore and climbed over 300 steps, on wooden stairways that clung to the edge of the steep cliff. Once arrived at the top, I found walking on the snow-covered roads that starlit, quiet night was a delight. Everyone who passed greeted me. I started a conversation with a miner, plying him with questions about the island. There were about 5000 inhabitants; wages were low and prices high. Many of the inhabitants had left the island to seek work elsewhere or to join the services, and there was much discontent with the government. The islanders felt that with such a wealth of ore on the island, a war in progress and so little demand for their ore, their interests were not being properly looked after. Compulsory education had only been in force for about three years. The local policeman's morning job was to get a list of absentees from the school and then round up the truants.

During our spare time we joined in some of the islanders' activities. These included dancing, skating, going to the pictures to see wild west films, and accepting invitations to spend evenings at people's homes. One day I was taken down the iron ore mine on a great wagon that was shackled to a heavy wire cable. The ride down lasted about seven minutes, and when we stopped we were two miles below the sea. The shift boss took me for a two-hour walk among a maze of tunnels and showed me the various operations used in mining iron ore: the pneumatic drills, the explosives, and the mechanical grabber that picked up the broken ore and placed it in small trucks that took the ore to the main shaft for transfer to the surface. It was a strange experience walking under the bed of the sea without any sense of direction, and in surroundings so foreign to me. I talked to some of the miners, and they seemed cheerful, independent and on an equal footing, and with no sign of deference to the boss. Our guide started work in the mine when he was nine and reckoned he had had 17 years of employment in the past 31 years. On the journey to the surface it grew steadily colder, and we had to duck to avoid icicles as we neared the intense cold on the surface. Many of our crew felt that the kindness, friendliness and hospitality of the islanders were far superior to what we generally experienced at a port. After discharging our ballast we went on to St John's, where we loaded a full cargo of newsprint.

St John's bound for London

On 9 February I was called early and went out into the bitter cold. I was grateful to snuggle into the warm hooded parka I had just bought second-hand from a local stevedore. After checking that the navigation equipment and steering gear were in order, I went to the stern to await orders to cast off. The tugs took our towropes and pulled us away from the dock into the black waters of the harbour. We headed out through the narrow gap between the high, snow-covered cliffs that flanked the port; then the tugs cast off, and the Pilot left.

Once we were clear of the harbour, I left my station aft and had breakfast. I was glad to be homeward bound, hoping we would be spared the gales and heavy seas that had broken up our convoy outward and made our lives miserable. I knew that German submarines had been reported off the Canadian coast, but they were an ever-present threat that I had learned to live with. After breakfast I relieved the Third Mate, who was on watch, so that he could have breakfast. By now we were proceeding along the channel, swept clear of mines, on our way to join a convoy. A salvage tug and a naval escort vessel accompanied us. As soon as the Third Mate returned to the bridge, I went into the chartroom to read over the convoy orders and lay off the courses that would enable us to join the main convoy.

Deeply engrossed in this work, I was suddenly interrupted by an explosion that shook the ship from truck to keel. I grabbed my coat and ran out on the bridge to see water, which had been blown high in the air, cascading down on the decks. Clouds of steam rose from a fractured steam pipe, and the *Kelmscott* was heeling over to starboard. My first thought was that we had struck a mine. Since the Captain and Third Mate were on the bridge, I went to the boat deck to be sure the boats were ready in case we had to abandon ship, and then mustered the crew. I made sure they all had life jackets, shared with them what I knew about what had happened, and told them not to leave the ship until ordered. I then assigned them different sections of the surrounding sea and told them to keep a sharp lookout for a periscope, since the submarine might be waiting for another opportunity to sink us. Reaching the stern, I found the gunners at their stations with the gun ready for use and gave them the same instructions. On the way back to the bridge, I saw the Steward and suggested he make a hot drink for all hands, because soon there would be no hot water left on the ship.

When I returned to the bridge I learned that the Chief Engineer had reported that the stokehold and engine room were flooding and it would not be long before the rising water would extinguish the fires in the boilers, the steam pressure would fall and the engine would slow down and stop. The steering gear was intact, and Captain Pugh had already turned the *Kelmscott* back towards St John's. The First Mate had leaned over the starboard side to look at the damage. He saw a jagged gaping hole that extended down below the waterline on the side of No. 3 hold, just forward of the stokehold and engine room. The explosion must have damaged the watertight bulkhead aft of No. 3 hold, allowing water to flow into the stokehold. He concluded that a torpedo had caused the damage, because a mine would have blown a hole in the bottom of the hull. We were fortunate to be carrying newsprint because it absorbed some of the shock of the torpedo, and would provide buoyancy until the paper became saturated with water. The Carpenter went round sounding the bilges in each hold to see if they were taking on water. He reported all holds were dry except No. 3.

We signalled our situation to the naval escort vessel. Shortly afterwards the rising water in the engine room caused our engine to slow and then stop as we lost steam. We signalled the tug and asked her to take us in tow. After what seemed an age of waiting – although I expect it was only a few minutes – the tug manoeuvred to windward of us and fired a rocket carrying a light line that landed on the fore deck. One of our sailors grabbed the line and took it up onto the forecastle. The Mate summoned everyone available to help haul the towrope aboard because we had no steam to power the windlass. The men pulled in three lines in succession, each attached to the other: first the light line, then a heavier coir floating rope and finally the towing hawser, the end of which had a loop that we placed over the bitts (heavy metal posts on deck used for fastening ropes or wires). The tug went ahead slowly, taking up the slack of the towrope, and then began towing us towards St John's. Shortly afterwards our electricity failed because the rising water flooded the generator. The sea was only moderate and the wind a fresh breeze, but unfortunately the temperature was down around zero Fahrenheit.

By then several naval vessels and aircraft had arrived and were circling in search of the submarine. At intervals of about half an hour we heard the sound of two muffled explosions and guessed that they might be distant depth charges. When the first shock was over there was little for us to do except wait and hope we would get back to port. Our four main holds were undamaged, the water was no longer rising in the engine room, and the tug was slowly but steadily moving us towards the land. It seemed we had a good chance of saving the *Kelmscott*.

About an hour and a half after the torpedo had struck us, a second explosion shook the *Kelmscott*, this time with still greater violence. Again, a great column of black smoke and water shot up several hundred feet into the air, and water rained down on the decks. At that time an aircraft was flying low directly above us, and it was thrown violently upward by the explosion. The plane nearly crashed into the sea before the pilot gained control. (It would have made history if the torpedo had downed the plane!) The *Kelmscott* was listing heavily, and the bow was sinking lower. The second torpedo hit about 50 feet forward of the first and tore open No. 2, our largest hold. The forward starboard lifeboat was blown to pieces and, just aft of it the second lifeboat had a side stove in.

The situation looked bad, and I heard the Old Man give orders to abandon ship. The crew lowered the two port boats, and men scrambled down the ropes and ladders and jumped into the boats. The Third Mate and the Cook were each put in charge of a boat. We told them to row well clear of the *Kelmscott* so they would not get caught in the downwash if the ship sank. For those for whom there was no room in the lifeboats, I released some of the emergency life rafts and, with help, brought them alongside, telling the remaining men to get onto them. One of the firemen fell into the sea: a young Ordinary Seaman dived in, pushed a raft across to him and pulled him out of the water. (Seventy years later, while searching the Web, I found that the seaman had been awarded the British Empire Medal for gallantry.) A great deal was happening, but I was too busy to see much of it. The behaviour of the crew varied from panic to bravery, from bawling and cursing to being quiet and following around anyone who would lead and give orders. The gun crew had remained standing by the gun, so I went aft and told them to leave the ship on one of the rafts.

Seven men stayed on the ship: the Captain, Mate and Fourth Engineer, a drunken Able Bodied Seaman, two gunners and myself. Because we needed an escape if the *Kelmscott* sank, I released the last life raft and pulled it round to the stern. We would not have had to stay on it long before being picked up by one of the circling naval vessels. On the bridge we gathered to assess the situation. The *Kelmscott* had settled lower, and the sea was lapping onto the deck forward on the starboard side. How long we would stay afloat was largely dependent on the newsprint. The large rolls that filled No. 2 hold would initially check the inrush of the sea and provide buoyancy. However, they would steadily absorb water, become waterlogged and thus lose their buoyancy. How long this would take we did not know. If the watertight bulkhead between No. 1 and No. 2 holds were damaged, water would flood into No. 1 hold, increasing the chance that the *Kelmscott* would sink.

I went off with Finney, our senior gunner, to No. 1 hold in order to find out. We made a sounding rod by cutting off the ends of a machine-gun ramrod. Through this hollow tube, we passed a piece of the rocket line that had been fired aboard. To get the sounding cap off, we had to use a cold chisel and hammer since the explosion had squashed the cap tight. To our relief, we found no water in the bilges. The Mate had signalled the tug and the escort vessel to let them know what had happened. The tug was still towing us, but at a greatly reduced speed because we were now much lower in the water. The escorts picked up the men in the lifeboats and rafts and took them ashore. As far as we knew, no lives had been lost.

The Old Man was on the bridge, and the Mate stood by forward in case the towrope broke. As there was nothing for me to do, I went in search of food. The galley fire was nearly out, so I stoked it up, and then investigated the pots and pans. Most of the food was ruined by dirt and salt water that had poured in through the skylight, but the soup was intact, since it had been covered with a lid. It provided the first course for dinner. There was roasted meat that had been taken out of the oven, so I put it back to warm. I then called Finney, one of the gunners, and using a fire axe, we went down into the food store, broke open the door and brought out some tinned peaches and cream. These provided the dessert. The only clean water was in a small tank in the galley, so we poured some of it into a kettle and put it on the fire to boil to make tea. Leaving the gunners to prepare and distribute the meal, I went out to see what was happening. The list of the ship seemed to have stabilized; she was down by the head and was lifting sluggishly to the waves. With the intense cold the water on the decks had frozen, making it hard to keep a footing.

Apart from the ship, my main concern was my clarinets. Not only were they my most valuable possessions, but also they were a source of great pleasure and provided me with an entrée to musical groups in ports we visited. In case the *Kelmscott* were to sink, I tied the clarinet case to a lifebuoy, went to the stern and floated the clarinets and lifebuoy on a long line close to the life raft that we planned to use. If we were to sink and had to use the raft, I could retrieve the clarinets. Somewhat later I had to haul the clarinets back aboard because the line to the raft had broken and the raft was lost. Leaving the clarinets in the galley, I went up on the boat deck to inspect the lifeboat that was our one remaining way of leaving *Kelmscott*. Though damaged, it would stay afloat if we had to leave. The falls (the block and tackles used to lower the lifeboat) were jammed, so I sent the gunners to fetch and load the rifles, so that in case of need we could shoot through them. Returning to the galley, I dried the clarinets and found they were not damaged. Some men were in the galley, the only warm place on the ship, so I gave them a short musical recital and then returned to the bridge.

While waiting with little to do, I was able to observe the behaviour of the Old Man. He had had a very hard time during the war, having been bombed or torpedoed I think five times. About 60 years old, he was showing the stress of his experiences. He mixed blasphemy in his abuse of the Germans and the men who had behaved badly on the *Kelmscott* with affection for his ship. He was cheerful in an aggressive, rough sort of way, and it was only later that he began showing his reaction to the shock by drinking. While the rest of us were busy he would leave the bridge and wander about the ship, noticing the queerest details, and then come and talk about them with the Mate and me. He reported, with great excitement, that his bathtub has been blown across his quarters and that a chip had been knocked out of one corner. A little later he came back having inspected the cadets' room and was indignant at the mess it was in

The Able Bodied Seaman who remained on board was somewhat drunk and at times very annoying. While the men were taking to the boats, he followed me about doing what he was told in a slightly fuddled manner. He refused to leave the ship when I told him to get into the boats, saying he was going to stay and look after me. He was in the way; I got rid of him by giving him my clarinets and telling him to stay aft and make sure they didn't get lost. He obeyed and stayed away until he had sobered up somewhat. The Mate was rather short-tempered, with a strong aversion to drunks, and I didn't want a row between them.

During periods when there was little to do, I thought about what had happened. I was confident we would survive, whether or not the *Kelmscott* sank. We had the damaged lifeboat, naval vessels that could pick us up were close by and, as a strong swimmer, I could survive for a short time in the water. Throughout the war I had known that we could be torpedoed at any time. Now it had happened, and we had escaped without the death and suffering that so often came in the wake of a torpedo, I found the activity, and having to deal with novel situations, exhilarating – unlike most of the time at sea when, apart from routine activities, little happened.

Several additional naval craft had come out from St John's, and a launch came alongside. Captain Slope, Chief of Naval Staff at St John's, came aboard, followed by a signalman. While he held a conference with the Old Man and the Mate I went with Finney, our gunner to sound No. 1 bilge to determine whether the forward bulkhead was holding. To our relief, we found no water in the bilges. By this time the water was lapping up onto the deck so there was only a foot or so of freeboard. In some places on deck, the force of expansion of the newsprint as it absorbed water had pushed out the sides of the ship and torn the deck and the sides of the ship apart. We reported our findings.

More tugs arrived. One of them brought out a pilot, who came aboard and reviewed the situation with the Old Man and Captain Slope while the rest of us went forward to make fast the additional tugs. There followed an hour or two of very heavy work, hauling ropes by hand as there was no steam to operate the windlass. Our difficulties were increased because many of the ropes were ice-covered and the ice on the deck made us slip. We lost count of the number of towropes that broke. We hadn't enough men to pull the broken ends back on board, so just had to cut them away with fire axes. Soon all our good ropes on deck had been sacrificed in this way, so we went down into the forepeak and slowly hauled out a new eight-inch manilla rope. Captain Slope had been busy on the bridge passing messages to the shore and nearby naval craft. Now he was up forward with us, hauling on ropes in a very sporting manner. The work enabled us to keep warm, as the sun by now was only a dull red ball close to the horizon. Every now and again great clouds would drift out from the land, and there were heavy snow squalls.

Our Pilot was a tall, elderly man with a great white walrus moustache and calm, kindly blue eyes. Nothing excited him. He spread peace of mind and confidence to everyone. As we drew nearer to the harbour, our confidence rose that we would get *Kelmscott* to safety. By the time we reached the narrow entrance to the harbour at about 7 p.m. it was nearly dark. The port authorities weren't going to allow the ship to enter, fearing she might sink and block up the harbour, but Captain Slope overruled them. Close inshore we were in smoother water. Additional tugs came alongside and we hauled still more ropes aboard and made them fast. Then slowly we moved into the harbour and approached the same pier we had left that morning. The Mate and I split our available manpower to go fore and aft to help us tie up the ship. He took three men forward, as he would have to handle the anchors, and I took one man aft. The task of tying up a ship without winches and with only two men would have been a tremendous undertaking, but to our relief a boat came off from the pier with six stevedores to help us. By now we were very tired but we kept going until the work was finished. We were all heartily thankful when the ship was finally secured to the pier. Even if she then sank, she only had a foot or two to go before touching the bottom, as we were drawing 30 feet of water forward.

Once we were alongside, a big shore party came aboard. While the Mate interviewed officials with the Old Man, I finished tying up the ship and got a gangway between the ship and shore. Then I went round with men from customs, sealing the places most liable to be pilfered. By nine o'clock we had done everything in our power. The dry dock officials had sent powerful pumps aboard to combat the water that had risen in the engine room over the boilers and engine tops. Arrangements had been made for our accommodation ashore, and leaving the *Kelmscott* in the hands of a customs guard, the Mate and I went ashore.

Looking back, we could see the chaotic state of the ship. The hatch covers on No. 2 and No. 3 holds had been blown off, and torn rolls of newsprint had been spewed up and were lying limply draped over derricks and winches. The heavy beams that held the hatch covers were lying scattered over the decks. Ventilator cowls, blown off by the explosion, lay battered and twisted where they had fallen. A tangled collection of ropes was hanging forlornly from the empty davits, and one of the davits was twisted as if a giant had been using it to vent his temper. Dirt and pools of frozen water gave the ship an unkempt, ragged appearance. Sticking up from the puddles of ice were debris and broken, buckled deck plates.

Many years after leaving the sea, I found out that the German submarine that torpedoed us was the U-845. She was commissioned on 1 May 1943, and after a training patrol started on her first operational patrol on 8 October 1943. We were the first ship she torpedoed. In the book *U-Boat Adventures* by Melanie Wiggins, the subsequent history of U-845 was given. On 14 February, an RAF plane attacked the U-845 in mid Atlantic with eight depth charges, causing the death of one crew member. Then on 10 March she was sunk by depth charges from two destroyers, a corvette and a frigate, with the loss of life of 10 lives and 45 survivors.

In my diary I reported that there were two unaccounted-for explosions at intervals of about half an hour between the times the two torpedoes struck us. In a report obtained later from the HMS *Gentian*, which was escorting us, it was stated: "At 1255 and 1308 two further heavy explosions were heard, but as no water disturbance was seen, it was considered that these were the results of torpedoes exploding at the end of their runs, or on the beach." Had those torpedoes hit us, we would probably have sunk.

At St John's, Newfoundland, February to March 1944

The Mate, the Third Mate and I were taken from the ship to Harvey's (our agents' office), where they made coffee that tasted superb. Everyone was talking about the happenings of the day. Lieutenant Hawkins and some of the shore staff from the rescue tugs, who were all Royal Naval Reserve officers, joined us, as Hawkins knew the Mate.

Eventually, the Mate and I got away and went by taxi to the hotel where we were to stay. After we had eaten, Lieutenant Hawkins and two other officers invited us round to their hotel. The Mate, Third Mate and I accepted, being too stimulated by the events of the day to go to sleep.

At the hotel we talked, while their playful puppy tore round barking and enjoying life immensely. Earlier in the war, Hawkins told us, he had been an officer in the merchant service, and while he was an officer on a tanker, the *San Demetrio*, she was set on fire and damaged by the guns of a German warship that had attacked their convoy. The Captain, expecting her to blow up as she had a cargo of aviation fuel, ordered "Abandon Ship", and the crew took to the two undamaged lifeboats. Hawkins was in one of the lifeboats overnight. Next day they sighted a ship and steered towards her in hopes of rescue. To their surprise, the ship was the one they had abandoned the previous day. He and the crew from the lifeboat boarded the ship and found the midship section completely gutted, and the navigation equipment and steering useless. The fire was still burning; they managed to put it out. They were able to start the engines that were undamaged and rig a jury rudder. Using the lifeboat compass, they headed east. After six days they sighted the Irish coast. They refused help, and on their own, with a naval escort, brought the ship round to the Firth of Clyde, saving both the ship and virtually all the cargo of aviation fuel.

When it came time to leave the hotel, the Third Mate began getting terrible pains in his side and lost the use of a leg. We were all very worried, but he was obstinate, saying it was nothing and refusing to see a doctor. However, we phoned for one without telling him. It turned out that he had broken a rib when he was thrown against the engine room telegraph by the second explosion. The Mate and I were sharing a room, and when we finally had baths and got to bed we were too tired to sleep. I lay awake with the events of the day rushing through my mind in a wild, kaleidoscopic manner, and when sleep came I was only to dream about hauling ropes and skidding about on icy decks.

When the Mate and I returned to the ship next morning stiff and tired, we felt a lot better after glimpsing the ship's masts and knowing she was still afloat. There wasn't much we could do aboard except take more precautions to prevent looting and try to keep warm. There were no facilities for cooking so we went to a café, where everyone stared at our tramp-like appearance because the only clothes we had were dirty and torn. That evening, the Mate and I turned in as soon as we finished tea, but we were again too tired to sleep. We lay awake until nearly midnight, when a maid came in to tell the Mate he was wanted on the phone by the Captain. Very reluctantly he went and soon came back, very angry, saying that the Old Man had asked him to go down to the ship because it was bumping badly against the quay. I offered to go with him but he wouldn't hear of it and went off by himself.

The following morning he was furious at having been turned out in the middle of the night, when there was little he could do except act as a scapegoat if anything went wrong. The outcome of the incident was a search for some party to take responsibility for the ship. Was it to be the Navy, the Ministry of War Transport, the dry dock officials, or the agents? These bodies all gave a glorious demonstration of "passing the buck". The outcome was simply that the Master was still responsible for the ship, and that a ship's representative must be aboard at all times.

From then on, the Mate and I took turns sleeping aboard. Within a day or two we had heat and light. We had no water or food, but we made friends with the captain of the tug alongside, and in exchange for some of our ship's stores his cook provided meals for us and buckets of hot water for washing. Our ship's cats were missing until we discovered them miserable, hungry, dirty and one of them wounded, down in the aft accommodation. We took them onto the tug, where the Cook kindly adopted them until their old home became habitable.

The pumps worked day and night to keep the *Kelmscott* afloat. An effort was made to remove enough newsprint to lighten her sufficiently to enable her to go into the dry dock. We found that soggy newsprint was as difficult to dispose of as dead bodies. Experts, after examining the paper, said that little of it could be salvaged. No one wanted the stuff dumped on his land, owing to the fire hazard when the paper dried. Officials racked their brains for a disposal strategy. The chauffeur of one of the dry dock directors solved the problem by suggesting that the paper be taken in motor trucks to the summit of Signal Hill, which guards the northern side of the entrance to St John's, and thrown over a precipice onto a small patch of wasteland that fringed the sea. Several more days were needed to obtain permission from the various authorities before the idea could be put into execution.

Knowing that a long spell of time lay ahead of us at St John's before we would again be at sea, and that that there would be little work for us to do on the ship, I looked for congenial activities. I had never had the opportunity to ski and hoped I might have the opportunity at St John's, where occasional good falls of snow were interspersed with rain, sleet and warmish weather. I bought a pair of skis, boots, harness and poles, but then the snow thawed and for nearly three weeks no snow fell. Just as I was beginning to curse myself for having made a foolish purchase, snow came. The hills round St John's weren't very high or steep, but I learned to descend a hill without falling and to gingerly make turns. I went with two sisters for a cross-country ski run along trails that led over frozen lakes and through pinewoods to the Newfoundland Hiking Club headquarters, a shack about five miles out of town. I loved the experience and the challenge of learning a new skill. I joined the public library, where I borrowed books, and attended morning sessions at the law courts to listen to cases that ranged from riotous comedy to pathetic tragedy. My clarinets, restored after their salt-water bath, enabled me to spend many evenings of music with the cathedral organist. We played at his house, and one evening at the empty cathedral, where the only light came from the organ loft and the moonlight, shining in white shafts onto the nave. Often, some of us from the *Kelmscott* went to dances and parties, and Hawkins and the officers of the naval rescue tug service introduced us to their friends. We got to know local people: dry dock officials, our shipping agents, customs personnel, and Ministry of War transport officials. We were even becoming quite passable gossips.

About three weeks after we'd got back to St John's, the *Kelmscott* was ready to enter the dry dock. We spent one of the coldest days of the winter standing about on deck shivering while tugs towed us to the flooded dock and nudged us in. There was still too much weight in the ship to allow the dock to be pumped dry, so some water was kept in to relieve the keel blocks of some of the weight. It was only when the water was pumped down that we were able to see fully the damage. Each hole torn open by a torpedo was big enough to allow a double-decker bus to be driven through the ship's side. Cracked rivets connected the two holes, and there was a mass of twisted frames, buckled plates and ragged edges. The next task was to take out the paper from the damaged holds, and this proved to be an enormous job. The rolls of paper had swelled with the water and most of it was solidly jammed together. All manner of ways were tried to remove the paper: axes, pneumatic drills, and finally dynamite.

About this time, the SS *Pachesham*, which also belonged to the International Newsprint Supply Company, arrived and the small amount of our newsprint that had remained undamaged, was transferred to her. One morning I was on the *Pachesham* seeing the Third Mate. He mentioned that he had met the captain of an American ship due to sail for the UK, whose First Mate had been taken to hospital with appendicitis and a replacement was needed. Later the same day the Mate from *Pachesham* mentioned the same thing. Half facetiously, I said "I think I'll take the job", and to my surprise he encouraged the idea. Then the Mate offered to introduce me to the captain of the American ship. Walking through St John's, we talked over the idea, and the more we talked, the more the idea took hold of me to make a trip on the American ship and return to the *Kelmscott* after she was repaired. He couldn't remember the name of the American ship and we were unable to find the captain at the Officers' Club. However, we learned that the ship was at anchor in the harbour. We went down to the jetty where launches plied to and from the ships, and we were soon aboard a big freighter called the *Mokihana*.

We found Captain Taylor in the mess room eating with a cheerful and untidy-looking bunch of officers. He took us up to his office and I explained why I had come. He seemed delighted, and jumped at my offer to sail with him as Chief Officer. I pointed out that I would have to obtain permission from the captain of the *Kelmscott* and that there might be regulations preventing my transferring from a British to an American ship. We agreed that I should return and get permission from my Captain, and then let Captain Taylor know his decision. I returned post haste to the *Kelmscott* to find that the Old Man had gone ashore and wouldn't be back until late that evening. So I went to the Old Colony Club Saturday evening dance, where I knew I would find all the people from whom I could get the information I needed. The first person I met was the manager of the dry dock, who estimated that it would take at least six months to repair the *Kelmscott*. One of the Ministry of War transport officials kindly enquired for me about immigration regulations governing a transfer from one ship to another, and he learned I would probably meet with no difficulties.

Next morning the Mate told me he had asked the Old Man about my going on the *Mokihana* and he had said that I could go. Strengthened with this news, I went to see the Old Man who told me my going on the *Mokihana* fitted his plans. He had been intending to sign off the Third Mate, because he didn't need three mates while the repairs were in progress. With my absence he wouldn't have to do this. I took this good news post haste to Captain Taylor, but one snag remained. He had earlier cabled New York for a replacement Chief Officer to be sent. Now he dispatched another cable cancelling the request. There was nothing to do but wait for a reply. I returned to the *Kelmscott* and arranged to meet Captain Taylor at the agents' office the following morning. Another period of suspense followed, until a messenger told me a replacement was on his way and due to arrive that afternoon. The news was a great disappointment, after nearly securing a trip to the UK, a Mate's berth and a salary many times greater than I then earned.

I went back to the *Kelmscott*, trying to pretend I wasn't disappointed, and began making plans for a long stay at St John's. Next day a boy came down from the shipping agents to tell me I was wanted at once. The Mate from New York had been sent by plane to Saint John, New Brunswick, instead of to St John's, Newfoundland, so the job was mine. It wasn't until I had signed off the *Kelmscott* and on to the *Mokihana* that I could believe my luck. That evening I packed my gear and said goodbye to the many friends I had made at St John's, and next morning, on 14 March, boarded the *Mokihana*.

CHAPTER 6

Mokihana

March to June 1944

Amermerican laws required that all officers on their merchant ships be US citizens. To get around this restriction, I was signed on as "Ordinary Seaman, acting First Mate". The *Mokihana* was a large cargo ship owned by the Matson Line, carrying a general cargo to England. As head of the deck department, I kept the 4 to 8 watch and was responsible for organizing the work of the deck crew. It quickly became apparent that the *Mokihana* was going to demand constant and undivided attention. For over a year she had had a new First Mate every voyage, and it was obvious that they had paid little attention to their work. What papers I could find in my cabin had all been thrown in a drawer in a heap with no attempt at order. The whole ship looked rusted and neglected, the storerooms were untidy, and when I arrived the forepeak had just been accidentally flooded.

For the first few weeks I just worked, ate and slept, and my thoughts rarely left the ship. After the long period of inactivity, the concentrated work was an interesting change. I had to learn American names for different parts of the ship and her equipment, and at first had difficulty in understanding the crew's conversation, humour and slang. It was my first experience of being on a ship where the only communication between the officers and men had to be through a union delegate, and there was a detailed set of union rules. On British ships, there was no union representative or book of rules, and little restriction on communication between the officers and the crew. I studied the union rules until I knew them almost by heart, and then met with the union delegate. I suggested there were two ways that we could work together. One was to stick rigidly to the union rules; the other was to live by the spirit of the rules, with give and take on both sides and mutual trust. I felt that the former way would lead to conflict and an unhappy ship and that the latter would be to our mutual advantage. If the crew wanted the latter way of working, there was a great deal to be done in bringing the ship back into shape, and if they worked well, I would pay them overtime. After discussing these options, the delegate talked with the crew and they agreed they would like the overtime and would be flexible about rules as long as it was to our mutual advantage.

Throughout the time I was with them we got along well together, and brought the ship back into good order. The Captain was concerned about the inexperience of the Second Mate and Third Mate, and when we were anywhere near land he required that either he or I be on the bridge. I did not mind the additional hours of being on duty, because it helped me to build up a good relationship with the Captain.

We went to Liverpool to discharge cargo, and while there I was able to go home on leave for a few days. From Liverpool we went to New York, where we learned that the ship was to go to San Francisco via the Panama Canal. Shortly after our arrival at New York, the shore Marine Superintendent came to see me, very angry at the amount of overtime that I had authorized. I took him round the ship, showed what we had done, and pointed out that if the work had been done by shore labour it would have cost the company a great deal more. His anger disappeared, and during the time in New York we became good friends. He asked me if I would stay on as First Mate on the voyage to San Francisco. There was nothing I would have liked more, as it would give me new places to visit and a continuation of high pay. But before I could accept the offer I had to find out the progress on the repairs to the *Kelmscott* and get the permission of her Captain and the British Consulate. I obtained these, with the understanding that the Matson Line, for whom I was working, would pay my expenses on the journey back from San Francisco to Newfoundland. When we reached San Francisco, I was again asked to stay on *Mokihana* for her next voyage across the Pacific. I was not sure whether the time I spent in charge of a watch on an American ship would count towards the watchkeeping time I needed before I could sit for my Master Mariner's certificate. I decided to leave after three months on the *Mokihana*, and signed off on 20 June 1944.

I had found the American crew took a lively interest in anything connected with the war at sea. Conversation often dealt with war experiences, convoys, submarines, torpedoes and bombing, whereas on British ships these subjects were rarely mentioned. The war at sea was still a novelty to the Americans, and there was not the same war tiredness as among British seamen.

On ships of both nationalities there were few signs of cultural or intellectual interest, although the British read more. In the officer's saloon, I was surprised at the amount of swearing and talk about sex compared to that on British ships, where there was very little. To my surprise I never experienced any resentment directed towards me as a British citizen aboard an American ship.

On Leave in the United States – 23 June to 1 August 1944

I was delayed leaving the *Mokihana* for the last time because the Chief Steward and the new Mate were happily drunk. I waited until the return of someone who could take responsibility for the ship, and then rushed to catch the ferry from San Francisco to Oakland, where the train to New York started from. Fortunately the train was delayed by over an hour, owing to lightning striking lines and breaking the electrical switching system of points.

In the evening an attendant came round and turned the seats into beds by swinging down the upper bunks that were folded against the wall. It made the carriage into a central passage flanked by two tiers of curtained sleeping compartments. These looked like a cross between large dog kennels and hiking tents. I slept badly, afraid of being shut in the confined space, and waking every few hours when the train stopped.

Finally I fell asleep and didn't wake until 9 a.m., when I realized that it was my 24th birthday. The train was in Nevada passing through sandy desert plains, with small scrub bushes the only vegetation. Every hour or two we passed small settlements of railway workers living in tiny wooden shacks clustered along the tracks. I was told that they were Mexicans, as no other labour was obtainable. Just before noon we stopped at Winnemucca, where everyone got out for a stroll and to buy milk and sandwiches at a café. It was the first time that I had seen waitresses wearing cowboy hats. We passed into Utah, where the line threaded its way around the hills standing out from the great salt flats, and late in the afternoon we stopped at Salt Lake City. At sunset I stood on the platform of the rear coach watching the mountains that looked as though they rose out of the sea. To while away the time, I found a man to play chess with, and read American history.

By next morning we were in Colorado. The train was climbing the Rockies, follow-ing a river. We passed small homesteads of log houses, some with water wheels over the river. There were horses and cattle, and the views were so rich and colourful that I was spellbound and could not leave the platform. We reached an altitude of 9000 feet and then the train wound its way down through scores of small tunnels. In front of the train we could make out a great plain; it was a wonderful day of sightseeing. I wished that I could get got off the train and stay in that land of peace, strength, and simplicity. After years of being at sea, the contrast of what I was seeing was especially poignant. We stopped at Denver and, tired of watching the scenery, I used the evening to play with some of the children on the train and learn something about how to hold babies, feed them with a bottle and change their diapers. The passengers were making friends and showed much kindness and thoughtfulness towards each other.

On 26 June we passed through rolling, rich prairie and farmland. That evening the train reached Chicago, where I had to change trains. I feared that it would be difficult to get a reservation on to New York, but was able to get a super stateroom through a military office. Soon after the train left, the comfortable stateroom made it easy to quickly fall asleep. I slept until noon, spending the last few hours of the trip wondering at the magnificence of the Hudson River. We arrived at New York at 4 p.m. and I found a hotel for the night.

I hoped that when I reached New York I might be able to visit the McCulloughs at their summer home in Vermont. Previously, when I had visited them at their New York home, they had hoped that one day I might be able to visit them in Vermont. First, though, I had to contact the Captain of the *Kelmscott* to find out how soon he wanted me back. I learned that it would be at least a month, so after obtaining clearance from Naval Control I phoned the McCulloughs. They urged me to come as soon as possible. I took the train to North Bennington, where Mr and Mrs McCullough met me at the station and drove me to their home. They had been instrumental in founding Benning-ton College for Women, had given the land and some of the buildings for the college and were trustees. To introduce me to the college, my hosts invited some of the girls to tea and for a swim in the pool beside their house. That evening I saw fireflies for the first time and was entranced.

After years of shipboard life with its monotony, social isolation and lack of intellectual stimulation, coming to the McCulloughs and all that they opened up for me was like a starving person given a delicious variety of food and drink. I entered the new experiences with wonder and enthusiasm, and spent much of my time at the college. The faculty and students were generous in letting me attend classes and share in their lives. To attend classes with gifted teachers was an exciting new experience. I went to dance, music and drama performances, and was included in parties and square dances. In the intervals between activities there was time to get to know some of the girls and share with them the various activities of the college. I was in the privileged and unusual position of going with the McCulloughs to meetings and social events of the trustees, being on friendly terms with the faculty and being accepted by the students. One evening I was at a formal dinner of the trustees, where the student waiting on me had been my companion the previous evening. I found the McCulloughs to be kind and thoughtful; they were good conversationalist, I enjoyed being with them, and it was like finding two grandparents. We had long talks about the history of their families and Vermont, and they had a lively interest in national and international affairs, books and antiques. When other visitors came to stay, there would be long and interesting conversations at dinner.

The McCulloughs had a polo pony called Intime on their farm, and I was eager to see if I could ride her. She turned out to be well-mannered, fast and nimble, and we got along well together. After I had been at Bennington for nearly three weeks someone told me that Peggy Black, a student at the college, had a horse. The next day I met her in a class and asked her if she would go for a ride with me. She kept her horse at a nearby farm, and we agreed on a meeting place. I don't remember the details of our first ride, but do remember that we got along very well together. It seemed only a day or two later that I was deeply in love with Peggy in a way that I had never been before, and she seemed to reciprocate my affection. I introduced her to the McCulloughs; they sensed our relationship and became very fond of her. A daughter of theirs had died not long before, and they seemed to give Peggy some of the love that they had had for that daughter. They suggested that she keep her horse in their barn beside Intime.

Each day I would attend Peg's classes, and when she was free we would go on long rides. Sometimes we would take a picnic and stop to eat in a meadow or high on a hillside with a view. There was an unused horse racetrack where we would sometimes race the horses. Above the McCulloughs' farm there was a track that wound through the woods, and when the horses were fresh we would gallop round this path, Intime seeming to revel in taking the sharp corners at top speed. Often the McCulloughs invited Peg over for dinner, so that we could spend our evenings together at their home, or if there was moonlight go for a night ride. If it grew past the time Peg was meant to be back at college, Mr McCullough would drive us to Peg's dorm by a back way, avoiding any security or staff that might report her late return. He seemed to get a childlike enjoyment in helping Peg break college rules while he was a trustee of the college. When not riding, we would share in the college activities, spend time with Peg's friends, swim or listen to music. Sometimes we would baby sit for college faculty.

It had been only about 10 days since I first met Peggy, but it was enough time for me to be certain that I wanted to marry her, and to learn that she felt the same way. The end of the college term, and the time for me to return to my ship, was approaching. Peggy asked her parents whether she could bring me home with her, and I think they must have been shocked that she had fallen in love with a sailor. Peg's father, Henry Black, taught at Harvard and her mother had been a college professor. They had a summer home at Tamworth, New Hampshire, where they had bought a farm on a hilltop. They drove over to Bennington to pick us up and were invited to dinner with the McCulloughs. At the dinner the McCulloughs told the Blacks about my grandparents and my family in England and, I think, slightly relieved the Blacks' concerns about me. The next day the Blacks drove Peg and me back to their farm in New Hampshire. I cannot remember whether, at that time, Peg and I had told the McCulloughs that we hoped to get married, but I do remember that they approved of and encouraged our relationship in every way.

I found it easy to get along with Peg's parents. Her father had been brought up on a farm in Vermont. Now he loved working around his summer place, planting a vegetable garden, raising chickens and looking after a horse that had been with the family for many years. I was able to stay with the Blacks for only three days. Part of the time I spent with Peg's father doing chores and odd jobs, which gave us a chance to get to know each other. I also had long talks with Peg's mother, to whom I took an instant liking. Peggy and I went for walks, swam at a nearby lake, visited a local craft fair and went for drives in their horse and buggy. When I had to leave it was hard to say good-bye, for it was wartime and we had no idea when or whether we would see each other again.

The Mokihana (*Reproduced with kind permission from the National Maritime Museum, Greenwich, London*)

left: *Author on the bridge*

below: *Peggy and author on wedding day*

CHAPTER 7

Return to the Kelmscott

3 August 1944

The temporary repairs of the torpedo damage to the *Kelmscott* had been completed when I rejoined the ship at St John's, Newfoundland. A week later we sailed, bound for Baltimore, where the permanent repairs were to be carried out. The voyage was uneventful until we ran into thick fog off the New Jersey coast. We reduced speed and were sounding our foghorn at regular intervals when we heard an approaching ship. When we saw her we altered course and she also altered course, but towards us rather than away. She hit us violently. Fortunately she ploughed into an empty forward hold so no one aboard was killed or injured. We were taking on water fast, so in order to bring the hole above water level we pumped water out of the forward tanks and into the aft tanks, with the effect of increasing the draft aft and raising the bow. When we radioed for help, tugs came out and took us in tow. After making very slow progress, we eventually reached Baltimore on 21 August. Later we learned that it was an American Liberty ship that hit us.

   With the damage caused by the torpedoes and the collision, it took some time for the shipping authorities to decide that it was worth repairing the *Kelmscott*. Since she would not be habitable, and we were in for a long stay, most of the crew was paid off and a skeleton crew, made up of the Captain and senior officers, was moved to the Lord Baltimore Hotel. My primary concern was to see Peggy as much as possible, and as there was little work for me to do on the *Kelmscott*, I was able to visit her almost every weekend. A maritime lawyer in New York was handling the legal matters connected with the collision. Our Captain did not want to make the trips from Baltimore to New York to help prepare the case. As he and I were on watch at the time of the collision, I was the person most suited to go in his place. On my first visit to the lawyer, I told him about Peggy and how we wanted to spend as much time as possible together. He was most sympathetic. To give Peg and me more time together, he asked the Captain to send me to New York for appointments with him on Thursdays. It was hardly worth my while to return to Baltimore for one day, so after seeing the lawyer on Thursday I would have a three-day weekend with Peg before travelling back to Baltimore during Sunday night.

Most of the weekends I stayed with the McCulloughs at Bennington. The visits spanned the period of autumn colouring in New England, which I had never seen. Sharing the experience with Peggy on our rides heightened the wonder of its glory. Many Vermont roads were still unpaved, and with few cars, they were perfect for horse-back riding. We spent hours exploring the region. One weekend we went on a 30-mile ride to Manchester. There we found an overnight stable for the horses, and a bed and breakfast for us. The McCulloughs used various means to enable Peggy to get leave from the college and stay at their house during my visits. During our evenings with them they would retire early in order to leave us on our own. One of my first presents to Peggy was a brooch made out of a fragment of a torpedo that hit the *Kelmscott* and had been twisted into an attractive abstract design.

We spent Thanksgiving at Peg's parents' home in Cambridge, Massachusetts. One weekend we stayed at the McCulloughs' New York home, and obtained tickets to attend a live broadcast of a concert conducted by Toscanini with the NBC symphony orchestra, a thrilling experience. I was eager that Peg should visit my colleagues from the *Kelmscott*, and when the repairs were nearly finished and the crew was back living on board, Peg came to Baltimore for a weekend. She was able to see where I lived, meet and get to know the Captain and the officers, and have some meals aboard. She quickly won the hearts of my colleagues.

Baltimore to London, via Saint John and Halifax

After nearly three months in Baltimore, the repairs to the *Kelmscott* were completed. We put to sea in December bound for Saint John, New Brunswick, where we were to load newsprint. From then until I left the sea my writing habits changed. The time I had spent on my diary was now devoted to writing to Peggy; my diary entries became irregular and were limited to important events. I continued to do my job, but the main focus of my thoughts was on my future with Peggy: where we would live, what vocations we would choose, the training we would need, and how we would pay for it. Because of this change I will select only the more outstanding events that occurred in the remaining voyages I made as Second Mate on the *Kelmscott*.

At Saint John, Peggy joined me for four days after the end of her college term. She spent time on board and again met the officers whom she had first met at Baltimore. Before we sailed, she returned to her family for Christmas. We went to Halifax, where we anchored to await sailing in convoy. On Christmas Day many of us gathered in the radio room to hear the King's annual Christmas speech. It was not so much what he said that was meaningful, but that widely scattered families would all be listening to the same voice, and thinking of one another.

Our Atlantic crossing was largely uneventful. We were bound with some other ships for London, so coming through the Western Approaches to Britain we split off the main convoy and went to Loch Ewe. There we formed up with other ships for the passage round the north of Scotland and down the east coast. Because we were vulnerable to air attacks, the Admiralty had placed two devices on the roof of the bridge intended to down dive-bombers. They were rockets, to which were attached long wire cables, and the idea was for us to fire off the rockets as a plane dived towards us. If all went according to plan, the up-stretched wires would catch the wings of the plane and bring it down in the sea. We were never able to test the idea, but the device occasionally went off accidentally, scaring everyone on the bridge. One night we were attacked by German torpedo boats and heard the exchange of fire between our escorts and the Germans, but no ship in the convoy was damaged. We reached our dock in London in January 1945, *Kelmscott* having been away for a year.

Remaining voyages on Kelmscott– *January to October 1945*

On my next voyage we returned to Saint John, New Brunswick, for a cargo of newsprint. While there, I was given leave to spend some days with Peggy. On both Atlantic crossings we sailed in convoy, and saw no enemy action. At the end of the voyage, when I had a few days' leave with my parents, I told them that Peggy and I wanted to get married. My mother counselled waiting until we were in a position to start a home and a family, while my father said he would support any decision I made, and would give no advice because he knew I would go my own way anyhow. They were saddened that they would see less of me, because in order to take leave in Canada to see Peggy I would have to take less home leave.

On my fifth voyage on the *Kelmscott* our destination was Botwood on the north coast of Newfoundland. On our outward passage on 10 May the news of the surrender of Germany came through, and at noon we listened to Churchill. There was little outward reflection of our feelings, but my emotions were so stirred that it was only with a conscious effort that I kept my face an impassive mask. I felt that as merchant seamen we were proud to move on, unaltered through war and peace, and the present lack of expression was the way we showed our pride. Over the radio came the descriptions and sounds of rejoicing in London, but here there was no change in the setting in which we had lived for so many years, with the convoy moving on so slowly, yet with a fatalistic persistence. There were the same grey clouds and the same angry sullen swell and white breaking seas that we had watched when the news came through of the fall of France, and the same unceasing round of watches that somehow gave us strength when we were in the Mediterranean in 1939, and Chamberlain announced over the radio that we were at war. Yet this seeming inevitable moving on and on had sometimes terrified me lest its strange fascination would grip me too firmly before I could escape the sea. I know now that I could and would escape. I thought of the joy that peace had brought to millions, and of the sorrow of those who had lost their homes and loved ones. That evening the "Old Man" invited us up to his cabin for a drink, and proposed a toast to the day for which we had waited so long. We stayed a while, but this was not a time in which we wanted to talk much, and we soon dispersed.

We reached our destination, Botwood, to load newsprint. Shortly after arrival I went ashore with Don Mossop, the wireless operator, to visit a friend of his who worked at a nearby flying boat base. No one was about. On the way back to the ship Mossop told me he had heard some mention of servicemen getting a free lift on the Royal Air Force trans-Atlantic flying boats that stopped at Botwood on their flights between Montreal and Britain. I had earlier written to Peggy that I would be unable to see her this voyage because of the difficulties of getting from Botwood. Now I realized that there might be a way to visit her. Later that day I found the officer in charge of the seaplane base and obtained his permission to go on the flying boat, due early next morning en route to Montreal. I obtained permission from the "Old Man" to go on 10 days' leave, on condition that I would be responsible for getting back in time to catch the ship before she sailed.

Early next morning I was ready and waiting for the arrival of the flying boat. I heard the sounds of her engines as she approached, but at the same time the base received a radio message saying that the clouds were too low for a safe landing and the plane was not stopping. This was a sickening disappointment. Not wanting to waste 10 days' leave I decided to go to Gander, a large airport about 40 miles away, in the hope of getting a plane ride to Montreal. I hitch-hiked on a train carrying logs to Grand Falls and caught a connecting train to Gander, then spent the night at Gander and next day was able to get a ride on a plane to Montreal. There I arranged to return on a flying boat to Botwood the following Thursday. I phoned Peggy to tell her that I would arrive at Bennington by train at 3 a.m. next morning. She was astonished, since I had written that I was not coming. Peg met me at the station and we spent what was left of the night at the McCulloughs. We decided to go to Peg's parents' farm at Tamworth, where we would get married the day after we arrived. After making plans, we got two hours, sleep.

The McCulloughs lent us their car, and after getting petrol coupons and wedding rings we set off over the mountains towards Tamworth, a journey of nearly 200 miles. We had to get a waiver for the five-day wait and blood test, and found a judge at Ossipee, New Hampshire, in the county where Tamworth was located. After hearing our case he granted the waiver and sent us to the Clerk of the court, who filled out the waiver and asked for the two-dollar fee. She told us that when the last couple had been asked for the two dollars the girl had turned to the man and said, "Do you think it is worth two dollars, dear?" With our intention of marriage now official, we phoned Peg's parents that we would be arriving shortly, and would they please find a minister because we planned to get married next day at their home. Mr Black, who had answered the phone, took this totally unexpected news with amazing calmness. We arrived at the farm early in the evening and after talking to the Blacks and having a meal went to bed, exhausted.

We were married on 27 May in front of the fire in the living room, with Peg's parents, her sister and two friends of the Blacks present. We had only two days before we had to begin the return journey. Peg's parents kindly went away, leaving us to look after the farm. When they returned they were amused to find us still asleep at 8.30 a.m. We had a glorious drive back across New England to Bennington, with the countryside looking its best in the warm sunshine after a night of rain. When we gave the McCulloughs our news they gave us a great welcome. Next day I had to leave by train on the return journey to the ship. The flying boat was delayed 24 hours leaving Montreal, because of bad weather, but the loading of newsprint on the *Kelmscott* had been delayed for the same reason so I got back to the ship the day before she sailed.

Shortly after returning, I gave a party for the captain and officers. I thanked Captain Pugh for his kindness in giving me leave, and the officers for the extra work that my absence had caused. Then they congratulated us and drank a toast to our happiness and marriage. I was shy of such gatherings, but it gave others pleasure and I think helped smooth away any annoyance or jealousy at my getting leave.

Our homeward passage was the first time in nearly six years that we were no longer at war. I wrote to Peggy:

> Outside the dusk is fast closing in, but my porthole is still open now the blackout is over. High on the foremast our bright navigation light shines out gladly to tell any approaching ships of our presence. The constant nightmare is over, of driving on through the nights in complete darkness and hoping that by keeping a good lookout, the grace of God, and good luck, we would not hit anything. We all feel a delight, childish in its intensity, at seeing the lights from the portholes streaming across the decks, and being able to sleep at night undressed with the fresh air blowing into our cabins. We know that now we can head straight for our destination, and the engines pulse with a fast happy beat. At last we are free from the irksome discipline of the convoys, with station keeping, zigzagging, and signalling between ships in the convoy with flags, Morse and sometimes semaphore. We no longer need to keep secret the ship's name, her destinations and our estimated times of arrivals and departures.

One of the peacetime pastimes of watchkeeping was signalling at night to passing ships to find out their names, where they were from and where bound. One night, using our signal lamp, I learning that a passing ship was a Norwegian, bound for New York. Their officer on watch learned that we were bound for Manchester, and signalled across that he wished he were aboard our ship because his wife lived in Manchester. I replied that I would gladly exchange places with him as my wife was near New York. We exchanged commiserations as long as we could see each other's signal lamp, and I enviously watched his receding stern light. The night and our feelings drew us strangely close, though we probably would never meet. Our voyage ended at Manchester, where we unloaded the newsprint.

I made three more voyages to Canada on the *Kelmscott* between June and October 1945 to load newsprint at Dalhousie on Chaleur Bay near the mouth of the St Lawrence River. On each, Peggy and I were able to spend a few days together. During these summer months the *Kelmscott* was kept running as hard as quick turn-rounds would allow, to take advantage of the good weather and make up for time lost due to the winter storms.

On the *Kelmscott* we had a series of incidents that, viewed collectively, may have been caused by the combination of accumulated wartime stress for seamen and the release of tension at the war's end. I believed that our shipping company recognized this situation because it began giving leave for entire voyages to its captains and senior officers. Signs of stress took various forms. There was a marked increase in the amount of malicious gossip, some of it directed towards Peg and me.

On one occasion I was on watch and fog had set in. The Old Man had been drinking, but because of the fog I asked him to come up on the bridge. The sailor on lookout duty stationed up on the bow was drunk and not capable of doing his job. I had given him a chance, but he fell asleep slumped over the rail on the forecastle head. I had arranged to have another man take over the lookout. The Old Man heard me and said that he would go forward and handle the affair himself. He went forward to the lookout and an extensive exercise in abuse, invective and blasphemy followed. The Old Man tried to get the lookout off the forecastle head but the man was offended and refused to budge. The Old Man then tried to throw him off by force, and a fight was just starting when a sailor working near by came over and stood between the enraged contestants until he was finally able to lead the lookout away. The Old Man came back to the bridge, bragging about how he had accomplished his task.

Quiet, broken only by the periodic blowing of the ship's whistle, lasted for just a few minutes before the offended lookout man came up on the bridge and challenged the Old Man to a fight. Words flew fast and furious on both sides and tempers were quickly rising, so I took what I thought was the most tactful course of action and gave a prolonged blast on the ship's whistle. The noise drowned any speech. I kept pulling the whistle lanyard until the angry gesticulations subsided. As soon as the whistle stopped, the anger and excitement began rising again. I held on as long as I dared and again called on the pacifying effect of the whistle. This sequence of events seemed doomed to continue indefinitely, as neither of the opposing parties saw the humour of the situation. I feared that if I was a shade late in next blowing the whistle I'd have a fight on my hands. Regretfully, I changed tactics and stood between the quarrellers until help arrived to take away the drunken lookout.

On another occasion the Third Mate came flying up on the bridge, as white as a sheet, almost crying. The First Mate had struck him, after giving him a torrent of verbal abuse about his laziness, incompetence and so on, and had threatened to give him a bad discharge that would prevent his getting his Mate's certificate. I told him to get written statements from any witnesses to the event (the Mate was very drunk), and come and see me after I came off watch. He later came to tell me that he had obtained witnesses' statements, which would be ample evidence to show the main office if the First Mate carried out his threat. Later, at an informal party on board, the Third Mate sat quietly drinking. His dislike for the First Mate must have been seething within, for suddenly he turned and socked him, good and hard, on the jaw. Immediately afterwards he was pathetically remorseful, saying, "You lousy swine. Come and beat me up. I deserve it, although you are a bastard."

These incidents did not make for a happy ship, and I was always worried that somehow I would be prevented from seeing Peggy. I could not remember any such scenes at sea during the wartime years. Fortunately the officers kept different watches, which limited their contact with each other.

At the end of the three voyages, we docked in London on 3 October 1945. One afternoon the Marine Superintendent asked me whether I would like to leave the *Kelmscott*, have leave until the 25th, and then join the *Pachesham*, also a newsprint carrier, as Second Mate. He told me that the ship would be visiting ports in Nova Scotia during the winter, meaning that I would be able to see Peggy, so I was delighted to make the move. It would also give me time with my parents, with whom I had spent little time since meeting Peggy, and time with my brother Olaf, whom I had not seen for five years. Being on the *Pachesham* would give me enough additional sea time to go ashore after one voyage to prepare and sit for the Master Mariner's exams and would get me away from the men with whom it had become so hard to live and work with.

Mixed with the pleasure of leaving the *Kelmscott* were regrets; it had been my home for two years and had provided me with some of the greatest experiences of my life. In retrospect, I thought that the company's offer had been made in line with their policy of giving ship's officers a voyage off to recover from wartime stress, and they probably had some knowledge of the situation on the *Kelmscott*. On 9 October I signed off the *Kelmscott* for the last time and went home on leave. It gave me time with my family, and to visit friends and go for long walks with my dog, Nansen. I slept long hours at night, probably the reaction to lost sleep while at sea. The rest and slow pace of life at home was wonderfully refreshing, and happily my leave was longer than expected because the *Pachesham* was delayed by gales.

CHAPTER 8

Pachesham

October 1945 to January 1946

A telegram arrived on 30 October ordering me to join the *Pachesham* at Manchester. On the journey down from Glasgow, I heard a point of view contrary to the one generally expressed by service people longing to be released. Three women were with me in the compartment, two in uniform and the other a civilian. The civilian, after struggling for some time to overcome her shyness, brought herself to start talking to the army women. She eagerly exchanged memories about the time she had been in the army, and then told about her present life back at home, which was an isolated farm. After the highly gregarious life in the army, she felt the farm was driving her crazy with its lack of crowds and organized entertainment. She had had to start organizing her life and thinking for herself, instead of always carrying out orders, having her food provided, and experiencing plenty of social life. The other two women listened sympathetically, as she talked out some of her pent-up misery.

When I reported aboard the *Pachesham*, the newsprint was being discharged. The *Pachesham* was an old ex-American ship, but my cabin was comfortable, with running water and a luxurious double bunk. The ship, which had been having engine trouble, was scheduled for fairly extensive repairs before she could sail.

Owing to the extensive repairs needed by the *Pachesham*, we did not get away to sea for 45 days. The delay gave me the opportunity to get to know Captain Lindsay, who was young, Scottish, easy going, and had a good reputation. His wife and child were living aboard while we were in port. The middle-aged Mate had been a prisoner of war in Germany for four and a half years after being torpedoed. His wife had had five months of suspense before she found out that he was alive and well. She was also living aboard. The Third Mate, who hailed from the Isle of Skye, spoke Gaelic more fluently than English. He was cheerful and had a wide variety of interests. It looked as though *Pachesham* would be a happy ship, after the interpersonal tensions aboard the *Kelmscott*.

One evening Captain Lindsay broached the subject of leave. He said, "I assume that you will be taking your leave on the other side with your wife?" Knowing about Peggy, he wanted us to have as much time together as possible. Later he suggested that Peggy join the ship in Sydney, sign on as Fourth Mate and go with us on the passage from Sydney to Saint John, New Brunswick, and then sign off. Then we could go on leave until the loading was finished. I sent Peggy a telegram telling her of this wonderful news and the best date I could predict when she should meet us at Sydney.

From our Marine Superintendent I had learned that there was an additional reason to be glad I had left the *Kelmscott*. On the voyage she was badly damaged by storms and had been diverted to Newfoundland for repairs. Had I been with her, I would have missed seeing Peggy.

I had hoped to spend Christmas with Peggy, but we were delayed by bad weather and did not reach Sydney until the following day. I hated Peg's being alone at her hotel on Christmas Day while we were still at sea. As soon as we docked I fetched her from the hotel and she came to live aboard. On New Year's Eve most of the crew went ashore to celebrate while we remained on board. The night watchman called me out because some of the crew had thought it would be fun to launch one of our life rafts and go for a paddle. They seemed insulated from the cold by the amount of alcohol in their blood. I got them back on board, and tied up the raft until we could get that back on board too. Around the midnight hour the crew began straggling back to the ship, and I stayed at the gangway to prevent people falling overboard and to help them to their bunks. The Canadian Navy League brought knitted blankets and winter clothing for the crew. Peggy was given the job of equitably distributing the gifts. She enriched mealtimes with her presence. The Captain signed Peg on as Fourth Mate, as he had promised, and it was wonderful for us to share the experience of being at sea together.

Shortly after we arrived at Saint John Peggy was signed off and I was given leave. Peg retrieved the car she had left at Saint John before going on by train to Sydney, and we set off to go skiing at North Conway, New Hampshire. Peggy was a very good skier, but I was not. My only advantage was that years of standing on rolling and pitching decks had given me a good sense of balance. I somewhat foolhardily tried the steep downhill slopes with little knowledge of how to turn, slow down or stop. My luck held for a while, but then I had a fall and severely twisted my knee. A local doctor put it in a cast and gave me crutches. So ended the skiing. Peg drove us to her parents' home in Cambridge, Massachusetts, and we spent a few days with them. While there, we bought presents of food and clothing to take home to my family, choosing food that had long been unattainable in Britain. Altogether we had 24 days together, before I had to return to the ship by train. It was my longest time with Peggy since we had first met 18 months earlier.

When I got back to the ship on crutches, everyone was in the saloon having dinner. They gave me a cheery welcome, without any of the malice or resentment that greeted such returns to the *Kelmscott*. I gave the Old Man the letter of thanks that Peg had written to him, and then had to answer a deluge of questions about my leave with Peg. Because so little of note occurs on a ship, the news that I gave them was hungrily received.

We sailed, bound for Manchester, on 25 January. My knee continued to be very painful. When on watch I wedged myself into a corner of the bridge. I asked if I could have one of our cadets on watch with me, and he was a great asset helping with the lookout. If all was quiet, I could rest my leg in the chartroom adjacent to the bridge, from where I could quickly be called out if needed. In exchange for his help I gave him some tutoring in navigation theory when we were off watch.

At the end of this voyage I would be going to the Glasgow Technical College to prepare for the Master Mariner's weeklong examinations, so I used my spare time for intensive study. We heard on the radio that the new Merchant Navy release groups had been announced; the groups included mine, removing the last doubt that I could now leave the sea. We reached Manchester, via the ship canal, and I signed off on 19 March.

CHAPTER 9

After I left the sea

The final entry in my discharge book read: "Discharged from Merchant Navy Reserve. Released on termination of war service. Certificate issued." Peggy and I had agreed that I should delay coming to join her in the States until I had obtained my Master's certificate. Getting the qualification might be helpful when it came to getting future jobs. The delay would also give me more time with my family before leaving Scotland. I prepared for the exams at the Glasgow Technical College, and shortly after passed the exams. Late in April I signed on the *Egidia* as a supernumerary Third Mate for a passage from Glasgow to New York. This was a gift from the Anchor Line for whom I had worked for nine years. Peggy met me in New York when the ship docked and we started our lives together in the United States.

To prevent an abrupt finish to this book, I will briefly outline my career since leaving the sea. While still at sea I had applied to become an undergraduate at Harvard University. I was accepted, and a month after joining Peggy in the States I started my studies at the age of 26. Three years later I graduated and went on to do graduate work at Cornell, and in 1956 I finished my studies with a PhD. I accepted a job offer to join the Association for the Aid of Crippled Children (AACC) in New York. They had long been a service organization, but recently had been left a large fortune by the husband of a board member who stipulated that the money be used to advance understanding of the causes and consequences of handicapping conditions, especially in children. The Board had decided to end direct services and to provide grants for research. My job was to develop a research grant programme with the understanding that I could also conduct my own research.

In 1969, after 13 years with the AACC, I accepted an invitation from Albert Einstein College of Medicine in New York to join their department of paediatrics as a professor and do research. I stayed there for 25 years until I retired, and since then have lived in a retirement community in New Hampshire.

Peggy and I had two sons while I was at Harvard and two daughters while I was at Cornell. In 1980 Peggy died of cancer. We had been married for 35 years, were very close and had shared many joys and sorrows. Her death left a deep void and sense of grief. One of Peggy's closest friends was Marion Lyman. Our families had known each other since some of our children were in nursery school together. Marion had lost her husband, and in 1983 we were married and are still together. I have been fortunate in living with two wonderful wives.

I have maintained my love of music and still play the clarinet in several ensembles. I still have a craving for physical exercise and at different times have played and competed in tennis, sailing, running and single sculling, which I still do. As a volunteer, I am a court-appointed advocate for children who have been abused and/or neglected. My habit of writing has continued. It was an essential part of my research work, and since retiring I have completed three books: *Twenty-Two Years* (which dealt with my previous research, *Lost and Found: The Search for my Family*), *A Childhood in Britain, 1927–1937* and this book.

—

During the 60 years that have passed since I left the sea, I have often thought about my good fortune while I was a seaman. There were some were escapes from misfortune. The first three ships that I sailed on were sunk shortly after I left them: *Elysia*, *Empire Beaver* and *Tahsinia*. If the *Kelmscott* had not been carrying a cargo of newsprint when we were torpedoed, I could well have lost my life. The newsprint cushioned the explosion of the torpedoes and kept the ship afloat because of its initial buoyancy. When the convoys I was in were attacked it was other ships that were sunk, and when we were in port during air raids none of the bombs struck us.

A chain of fortunate and fortuitous events that led to my meeting and marrying Peggy. Some of the links were the torpedoes that struck the *Kelmscott*, the events that led up to and included my voyages as Mate on the *Mokihana*, the friendship of my grandparents with the McCulloughs, which enabled me to get to know the McCulloughs and go to North Bennington, their connection with the Bennington College, and my horseback riding at the McCulloughs' farm that led to my meeting Peggy. A friend once told me that if I fell down a sewer I would come up with a gold watch in each hand.

The experiences I had at sea helped me develop in many ways. The deprivations imposed by confinement in ships for long periods developed in me a craving for all the opportunities that life ashore provided, and since leaving the sea I have tried to live as fully as possible. Prior to going to sea I had poor study habits and little confidence in my academic ability. While at sea the correspondence courses I took in preparation for the nautical exams were an incentive to study because I wanted to get ahead. I had little or no help from others so had to work out problems on my own. I learned to concentrate in order to shut out the distraction of the ship's noise and her movements in bad weather, and to overcome the lethargy brought on by extreme heat and humidity. I read widely while at sea, and books served as an escape from shipboard life. I could lose myself in a book and concentrate on it. My diary writing improved my skills as a writer. From these experiences I gained the confidence to apply to Harvard. My acceptance there was probably partly due to my nautical certificates because they gave me course credits towards my degree.

My sea experiences held me in good stead in my subsequent career as a research worker and writer, where for much of my time I worked alone. I had become accustomed to solitude during the hours on watch at sea and often when off watch, so was well prepared.

At sea I gained valuable experience in organization, administration and leadership, and these skills have since served me well. During emergencies I could not, as a ship's officer, allow my fear to interfere with what I was doing, and it was important to remain outwardly calm because if I showed any signs of fear or panic it could spread among the men I was supervising. Overt conflict among the officers and captain could be damaging to morale and possibly to the safety of the ship. For these reasons it was important for me to learn to control my feelings. I believe this has contributed to my being reserved and to restrict outward displays of emotion.

I did not choose my shipmates. Many were people that I would otherwise not have selected as companions. Having to get along with them, I learned that if I did not prejudge, was curious, and showed interest in their lives, I could learn from their experiences and find them interesting. At sea I had no opportunity to socialize in large gatherings, which I would probably have had if I had lived ashore. These experiences have helped me to relate in small groups with one or two other people, but have made me shy and uncomfortable in large gatherings.

Sometimes I was captivated by life as a seaman, and sometimes I hated it, but I will always be grateful for the experiences it gave me.